JOHN DALY:
Wild Thing

JOHN DALY: Wild Thing

William Wartman

AURUM PRESS

First published in Great Britain 1996
by Aurum Press Ltd, 25 Bedford Avenue, London WC1B 3AT
© 1996 by William Wartman

Published by arrangement with HarperCollins*Publishers*,
10 East 53rd Street, New York, New York 10022

A catalogue record for this book is available
from the British Library.

ISBN 1 85410 443 8

10 9 8 7 6 5 4 3 2 1

2000 1999 1998 1997 1996

Printed and bound in Great Britain by Hartnolls Ltd, Bodmin

Acknowledgments

I would like to express my appreciation to all those who made themselves available for interviews for this book, as well as to the following people, who contributed significantly to my research: Maggie Hassett, in the computer database center at the Free Library of Philadelphia, and everyone in the newspaper department there; Gary Hayden, in Texas; Patti Moran, at the U.S. Golf Association; Donna Slawsky, in the Harper-Collins library; and Joe Wartman, at Berkeley.

Deb Conte, Ph.D., and Robert Partridge, M.D., helped with information on psychology, addiction, and recovery. Mike Rugg, at Cobbs Creek Golf Club, illuminated the role of the club pro, and Mark Soltau explained the California swing of the tour. Emma Edmunds was a source on the South. The Dursos assisted with the logistics of transportation. David Bradley was a sounding board.

Carolyn Marino, my editor, was a font of enthusiasm and forbearance. Geoff Hannell conceived the idea, and Ed Breslin, my friend and first editor, made the introduction.

Contents

The Swing

The Catholic kids always sneered when a Protestant transferred into their school—especially one who, like John Daly, was preceded by street talk. The word around Jefferson City, Missouri, in 1982 was that Daly, the new kid in town, was better than any boy golfer they'd ever seen. They said that at fifteen he routinely shot par, something most other golfers only fantasized about.

The guys on the golf team at Helias High School had one thing to say about Daly's purported scores: Yeah, right. Jefferson City, nestled in rolling farmland off I–70 on the way from St. Louis to Kansas City, had been growing in recent years, and so was Helias. They had added a fine-arts wing, and bulldozers were about to tear up Swifts Highway to create more parking out front. Transfer students had been blowing into Helias as regularly as storms off the Great Plains, bringing the student body to eight hundred. But just as the neighboring Ozark Mountains tempered those squalls, the boys of the Show Me State knew how to bring a new rooster down to size. They took him out and stuck a driver in his hands.

1

So when John Daly stepped to the first tee during his opening day of practice for the Helias Crusaders golf team, there were dozens of furtive glances shooting about. What a guy showed you on the first tee was as important a measure of him as what you'd see in the showers later on, but in both cases, it was a situation where you didn't want to gawk.

As Daly drew his club back, Ray Hentges, the Helias golf coach, noticed right off how flexible the kid was. He contorted his shoulders around like a track and field guy about to put the shot. Hentges was impressed by that, and he took it as a sign that his crosstown rival over at Jefferson City High School hadn't been pulling his chain about this new boy.

Hentges had first heard about Daly when the kid was a student at Jefferson City High School, Helias's much larger public-school counterpart. The golf coach there was bragging on the amazing golfer who had just transferred in, and Hentges could only chalk it up as another of the countless advantages the taxpayer-supported school seemed to have over his parochial institution.

Then, only days later, the Helias principal, Jim Rackers, sidled up to Hentges in the hall, struggling to suppress a very self-satisfied grin. What, the principal inquired, was the ineligibility period for participation in athletics when a student transferred to a new school after leaving his previous school before he could memorize his locker combination?

Hentges said he thought it was a year, but asked what the deal was. "Even as we speak," Rackers said, "John Daly's mother, Lou, is in the office transferring John and his older brother, James, to Helias." Although the Dalys were Episcopalian, Mrs. Daly told Rackers that John, her fearsome golfer son, had been intimidated by the twenty-four hundred students at Jefferson City High and had bolted in three days. After a childhood spent in small towns and even smaller schools, John Daly, a shy and slightly built boy, wasn't comfortable with all that bustle.

2

This was not the first time in his itinerant childhood that Daly had spent less than a week of the school year with one class. The rootlessness had begun in Sacramento, California, where John's father, Jim, had gotten into the business of doing construction work at nuclear power plants that were being built or overhauled. When John was five, his father signed on with the Arkansas Nuclear One plant, and the Dalys moved to a tiny burg in west-central Arkansas called Dardanelle.

The South wasn't alien turf to the Dalys. Their ancestors had emigrated from Ireland through Kentucky and into Arkansas several generations before. John's grandfather had grown up in Arkansas, and other relatives still resided in the state. Nonetheless, it would be difficult for anyone to remain a stranger for long in a town like Dardanelle. It was an isolated farming and poultry-processing hamlet—the kind of place where if you went to the store, other people knew. And when they spotted you on the road, they'd raise their left index finger—and only their finger—off the steering wheel in salute.

Little Rock sat eighty miles to the east, but the state capital might as well have been eight thousand miles away, for all the impact it had on life in Dardanelle. People were so unassuming there that no one minded—or perhaps even noticed—that a boundary sign at the town's southern edge put the population at 3,684, while those elsewhere around the perimeter proclaimed it to be 3,621.

Dardanelle had the disheveled look towns take on when people work the land as well as live on it. Resources were limited, and tomorrow's prospects always had the worrisome feel of a promise you extracted under duress. The folks who lived there had never been given much, and so they took nothing for granted. They believed that if you wanted a satisfying life, then you had to master the art of getting by—of plucking maximum utility from what you had, and improvising like crazy for whatever else you might want.

Young John grasped that maxim early in life, as the Dalys were settling in a valley called Wildcat Hollow, across the way from Lake Dardanelle. Being the youngest of three children in a family in which people mostly went their own way, and living in a town that was overwhelmingly populated by adults, John discovered that if he was going to have any fun, it was up to him to devise it. He was also going to have to do it quietly when his father was around.

Jim Daly was a hard-working man, and his schedule was irregular. He was away sometimes, but other times he'd be working nights and sleeping days. Regardless of his timetable, he was a man who enjoyed a beverage with bite when he came home from work. Jack Daniel's was his brand.

Although John didn't spend a lot of time with his father, he discovered there were a multitude of things an obstreperous boy could do to invoke the man's wrath when he was in the wrong mood. The unpredictability of all this was daunting enough that John grew up a very careful child. He was especially cautious about making people mad.

Perhaps it was inevitable, then, that Daly would come to make his way down Highway 22 to the serenity of the Bay Ridge Boat and Golf Club at an early age. He had been slapping golf balls around with cut-down clubs since he was in diapers, but the game took on a larger purpose when he fell under the spell of the first and only hero of his life: Jack Nicklaus.

In the early 1970s, Jack Nicklaus amassed new golf records more quickly than sportswriters could comment on them. He initiated his 1972 season by winning the Bing Crosby National Pro-Am, which was his fifth victory in the last six tournaments he had entered. Later that year he won both the Masters and the U.S. Open after either leading or sharing the lead in every round of both tournaments, something no one else had ever done.

Nicklaus tied golfing great Bobby Jones's record of thirteen career wins in golf's major championships—the Masters, the

U.S. Open, the British Open, and the PGA Championship—that year, although that record, too, would soon fall. Nicklaus's dominance of the majors was such that he was considered among the favorites in every one he entered. The writers always noted the one factor that made Nicklaus such a contender—his seemingly superhuman length off the tee, which enabled him to drive the ball past the devilish trouble spots that were designed into courses that hosted the majors.

Nicklaus's other salient characteristic at the time John Daly discovered him on TV was his enormous, and newfound, popularity with the galleries. Golf fans had come to forgive Nicklaus for displacing the much-loved Arnold Palmer as the top golfer on the PGA Tour, and Nicklaus had warmed to the fans in turn.

After spending the sixties as a hefty, unsmiling, crew-cut, Teutonic interloper who was sometimes blatantly harassed on the course by Palmer's fans, Nicklaus had, in the parlance of the times, gotten with it. He let his hair and sideburns grow, lost weight, and spruced up his wardrobe with modish shirts with elephantine collars and pants with wide white patent-leather belts. Although he insisted all of this was a coincidence and not an effort to appease the galleries, Nicklaus also tried to smile more inside the ropes.

The one thing he never changed, though, was the way he played golf. Nicklaus was as fearless and steadfast a competitor as had ever laced up a pair of spikes. He not only wanted to win every tournament he entered, he preferred to win them decisively. He wanted to hit the longest ball off the tee, and when he was hot, he was going to gun for the flag whenever possible.

That attitude was palpable and, combined with Nicklaus's new persona, it eventually won him the devotion of golf fans. On a good day at an important tournament, there would be more people scrambling around a golf course after Jack Nicklaus than the entire population of Dardanelle. This didn't escape the notice of one of that town's younger residents.

Growing up, all John Daly ever wanted in life was to be on the PGA Tour and have people follow him like Jack Nicklaus. Whereas other peewee golfers imagined themselves capturing the U.S. Open trophy when they played, Daly imagined himself winning the adulation of a teeming gallery.

As a first step toward realizing that dream, Daly studied Nicklaus's swing on TV. He saw that it was long and that Nicklaus got his hands up high over his shoulders before he attacked the ball. He hit the ball so hard that the tee would be yanked from the ground in one piece, before it somersaulted back to earth.

When Daly was seven or eight, if Nicklaus wasn't in a tournament that was being televised, Daly wouldn't watch. He'd go outside and practice his version of the dominating Nicklaus swing. He'd roam the fairways at Bay Ridge all weekend, and before and after school, playing by himself unless there were some indulgent adults around who would let a kid tag along. To those who saw him, he looked amazingly carefree.

Within a few years, what Daly learned from watching Jack Nicklaus on TV enabled him to act out golf's Oedipal fantasy. By the time he was nine years old, John Daly could murder his father on the golf course.

Although he might not enjoy such a thrashing, Jim Daly could at least salve his wounded ego with paternal pride at the precociousness of his offspring. That was not the case with other grown men who were bested by a kid whose voice hadn't changed.

From the time John was ten until his second day of ninth grade, the Dalys lived in Locust Grove, Virginia. John played his golf at the Lake of the Woods course in Fredericksburg, and when he was thirteen years old he won the club spring championship. Not the junior championship. *The* club championship, defeating every adult golfer who entered the competition. The men were so furious and humiliated at being battered by a thirteen-year-old that they rewrote the rules. Henceforth, no one under eighteen could enter the tournament—giving the grown-ups a lock on the trophy for the next five years.

The men of Lake of the Woods need not have worried, though, as the Dalys were soon on the road again, this time to Zachary, Louisiana. John completed ninth grade there, and half of tenth, until his father found work at the nuclear power plant that was under construction in Reform, Missouri, forty miles south of Jefferson City.

The family bought a house on Joseph Road, out on the far western edge of Jefferson City, where the first small bits of farmland were being transformed into subdivisions. In a state that uses letters as highway designations, the Dalys were on the other side of Highway X. Jefferson City was the state capital, and there was a prison there, so the government employees outnumbered the farmers—in sheer numbers if not in acreage occupied.

It was a bona fide city of 34,000, although this was still the Midwest. People were friendly, and children tended not to flee from their families when they became adults. Folks watched out for one another, too.

That's what happened when Ray Hentges, the Helias golf coach, went to the Missouri State High School Activities Association about John Daly's eligibility for his golf team. The rules clearly stated that a transfer student had to spend a year on the bench—to avoid the poaching of athletes by rival coaches.

But Daly had spent only three days at the other school, and, well, who knows? It was Ray Hentges asking, and he was a respected man in Missouri high school athletics. After eighteen years of coaching football at Helias, Hentges had compiled an estimable record of 187 wins against only 62 losses.

Football generated a lot of excitement and pride at Helias,

but the wrestling team, which Hentges didn't coach, was beginning to steal some of its thunder. Hentges's golf teams had never been much, but Ray's fifteen-year-old son, Chris, was an exceptional golfer, and if this John Daly joined him on the team . . . Ray, a mild-mannered but dogged man, didn't want to jump ahead and start talking about a state championship. You do that, you can jinx the whole thing. But he wasn't going to rule anything out, either.

That's why he smiled broadly when the state association bent the rules and said John Daly would only have to sit out three matches in 1982. So that was straightened out, and now Daly was on the first tee during his initial practice session, and he had extended his backswing until his driver was way beyond parallel to the ground—as if he were preparing to unleash a sledgehammer at a rock.

A couple of guys on the team glanced at each other ("Hey, where'd he learn that?"), then focused in to see Daly whip his driver around as though it had been launched from a catapult. Everyone was transfixed waiting for the thwack of club against ball, but it never came.

Instead, there was a muted chirp as his driver glanced over the top of the ball and sent it screaming through the grass like a mutant worm. Stone-cold topped it. Hell, it must have gone what—eighty yards?

"That's all right, John," the guys said. "No big deal. Do the same thing all the time. Don't worry about it."

Nobody was callous enough to smile, but there are things you notice and things you don't. Maybe you wonder to yourself: "So this is the dude who shoots par? I think not." And on this day the show-me boys of the Helias Crusaders golf team were right. Daly never did come storming back to shoot par.

Actually, he finished at one under.

2

Dough Boy

A few months later, while John Daly and the guys from the Helias golf team were still getting to know each other, a bunch of them were standing around in Brad Struttmann's front yard. Struttmann was a sophomore, like Daly, and his family's house was just up the street from the Hough Park golf course, where the team had a practice session scheduled that afternoon. They were just hanging out, playing a little grab-ass, the way guys are apt to before reluctantly performing any activity that has been mandated by an adult.

While the others were talking, Daly looked down the peaceful residential street toward Hough Park and judged that he was positioned only a long and exceedingly straight tee shot away from the course. Standing there surrounded by his new teammates, Daly was overcome by an irresistible impulse, one that combined the adrenaline surge of real danger with the ego boost of flaunting your athletic prowess.

He silently yanked his driver from his golf bag, stuck a teed ball in Struttmann's front lawn, and took aim down the street—past the houses and the cars and the sparkling vertical lakes of glass. As he addressed the ball and waggled his club behind it, Daly looked up and bet his buddies that he could rip a drive over the yards, around the utility poles and wires, and clean to the course without breaking anything or killing anyone.

"No!" Struttmann yelled. "Are you crazy? Don't. John, stop."

But Daly ignored the pleas and smashed the ball anyway, while his friends froze in terror. He whistled it by the houses and cars of Struttmann's neighbors and through to the park. The guys from the golf team screamed in relief when the ball rolled to a stop, then they cleared out before anyone could come charging out of a house threatening to call the cops.

They weren't so lucky a few months later, during a round at the Jefferson City Country Club, where John, Brad, and Chris Hentges, the coach's son, had junior memberships. The threesome waited on the fourth tee one afternoon for what seemed like an eternity. Up ahead, a pair of ladies playing out of a golf cart were taking their time advancing their balls. Finally the women cleared the bend on the 400-yard hole that doglegged to the left. Daly got to his feet, gave the women a few minutes to reach the green, then ripped a big, hooking drive that disappeared around the turn on the fairway. His ball bounced once and smacked into the women's cart with a resounding thwack.

The golf cart came roaring back toward the tee in moments, spewing a trail of dust. The two women inside were hollering, and one of them was holding up the golf ball and shaking it. The women asked whose ball it was, and when Daly owned up, they lectured him on the damage he could have done, on golf etiquette, on respect for his elders, and on everything that every disapproving mother has ever found lacking in another woman's son. When they drove off, Daly smiled sheepishly.

Although he was only a kid, Daly was always in a hurry on the golf course. But this didn't affect his performance. In his sophomore year at Helias he had set a new school record of four under par for a nine-hole match. His season stroke average on a par 35 course was 36.62. He placed third individually at the state tournament, after leading the school team to district and conference championships and a 66–7 record.

Daly's academic performance was a far different matter. While his friends might have worried about their grades and the connections their parents made between those grades and their futures, John didn't, and his report cards reflected this. Daly knew where he was going. He told everyone who would listen that he would be playing professional golf—and that they didn't check your SAT scores on the PGA Tour.

Although teenagers have always boasted to their friends, and buddies go along because that is what friends are supposed to do, no one at Helias High School ever doubted what Daly said about golf. He was so talented, focused, and driven, they told themselves, that if he couldn't make it, no one could.

What set Daly apart from his peers was not his showy shots from the tee, which, despite his extended swing, were only slightly longer than those of the other kids on the golf team. It was his putting that distinguished him. Daly routinely made the ten- to twenty-footers that the other teenagers seldom dropped. He also practiced obsessively, and therefore his game constantly improved.

Jim Daly was doing well financially, and he didn't require his son to work in the summer. John's routine was to play eighteen holes in the morning before going home for lunch. Then he'd shoot another eighteen in the afternoon before breaking for dinner. At night he'd go to the driving range and hit balls for two hours. With most of his golf friends holding down jobs, Daly played much of this golf by himself.

If Chris Hentges and Brad Struttmann were able to come along, John would often show his gratitude by giving them golf balls or buying them lunch. He loved to eat, and they would have contests to see who could consume the most food in one setting at McDonald's. Daly always won. It wasn't uncommon for him to spend $6 to $8 on himself during one visit.

When the golf team played in a tournament, the coaches often brought up the rear, playing the course behind their students. Helias's coach, Ray Hentges, had a standing offer to buy the dinner of any of his boys who bettered his score, when they stopped at McDonald's on the way home. Hentges occasionally had to buy a Big Mac for someone other than Daly, but John beat him routinely. With Daly's appetite becoming insatiable, he started having a serious impact on the coach's income. Ray Hentges was finally forced to enact the glutton rule: His contribution to the cost of dinner was henceforth capped at $3.

Daly's hunger was allowed free rein at home, and it was there that he acquired a taste for a unique culinary creation that became his comfort food and talisman: the combination of chocolate and dough. Although many southerners include biscuits and gravy in their breakfasts, John found that this didn't satisfy his considerable craving for sweets. So he replaced conventional gravy with Daly gravy: melted chocolate bars.

Given his innate impatience, Daly favored heat-and-serve biscuits that could be prepared in scant minutes from the tubes of refrigerated dough Lou Daly brought home from the supermarket. His requirements for chocolate were that it be thick, rich, and able to cloak a hot biscuit to a tooth-aching thickness.

Especially in the morning, Daly ate his chocolate-covered biscuits one after another, as though they were oversized frosted cornflakes. When Brad Struttmann and Chris Hentges slept over at the Dalys' one night before a morning golf match they were all playing in, chocolate-covered biscuits were on the breakfast menu. As Brad and Chris nibbled on one, John wolfed down half a dozen.

"These are so rich," Brad said to John. "How can you eat so many?"

"I have to," he said. "They're my good-luck food. Whenever I eat a mess of them in the morning, I always play well that day."

Daly gained weight so quickly after he moved to Jefferson City that it raised some eyebrows. A significant portion of Daly's calories were coming from the carbohydrates and fats of biscuits, hamburgers, and tacos, but another large chunk was coming from the sugars of alcohol.

John Daly lived in two worlds in Jefferson City. One was populated by his golfing friends, such as Chris Hentges, who couldn't have been a more unlikely companion. Hentges was every midwestern family's dream son. He was polite, earnest, dutiful, God-fearing, handsome, and athletically gifted.

At six feet and 216 rock-solid pounds in high school, Chris set new records almost every week as the fullback on the football team. He was a highly competitive wrestler, and on the golf team he was second in ability only to Daly. By the time he graduated from high school, he would be voted the best student athlete in the state of Missouri and make honorable mention as a high school all-American.

Even more central to his character was his role as the coach's son at a Catholic high school in a family-oriented midwestern town. Chris's father taught at the school he attended, and had for years. Given the moral uprightness of his upbringing and the long shadow cast by his father, guys like Chris Hentges either become the straightest of arrows, or they spend their lives in habitual rebellion. Hentges chose the former path.

Away from the golf team and the likes of Hentges, John Daly ran with a crowd of football players who disregarded the strict prohibition against athletes drinking while they were in training. If you had the money, beer was easy to come by in Jefferson City, and John Daly began consuming beer with the same gluttony with which he consumed tacos. By the time he was a junior in high school, his alcohol tolerance was such that he could drink almost a case of beer in one sitting.

Jim Daly was spending a lot of time on the road, working at a power plant in Ottawa, Kansas, and his wife, Lou, often accompanied him on these trips. This left John and his older brother, James, home alone. The parentless Daly household soon became party central in Jefferson City. A lot of drinking went on at those parties, and as with so many things in his life, John Daly took it to extremes.

Daly was nervous around girls, and he liked the courage alcohol gave him. Unfortunately, he decided to fall in love with a girl who didn't like beer or people who drank it. They dated on and off, but it was always the same story: The more Daly chased her, the faster she was to break his heart. It seemed as though each time she broke a date or ended the relationship yet again, Daly would drink a little more. More than once he became depressed and started crying over how this girl had hurt him. Some of the guys from the football team who were around when this happened would get edgy and slip away.

Daly managed to move between these two worlds adroitly, raising hell with the party crowd but still devoting most of his time to playing serious golf. In a pattern that would repeat itself throughout the next dozen years of his life, people who liked John and were awed by his golfing ability crossed their fingers and hoped he would outgrow the rest.

What Chris Hentges shared with John Daly was the boyhood dream of playing professional sports. In Hentges's case, it was starring in the National Football League. He was the archetypal high school football hero, and it didn't require a fertile imagination to envision the thunderous stadiums and praise-filled headlines rolling on for another two decades. But in the quiet moments away from the solicitous Helias parents and alumni and the deferential kids at school, Hentges knew that he had no chance of ever making it in the pros. As good as he was, he didn't have quite enough talent, or the requisite all-consuming drive, to compete for a living against the very best in the world.

John Daly, however, seemed to have both talent and drive in excess. So although Chris Hentges didn't approve of Daly's lifestyle, he respected Daly's belief that he was going to live the dream. To express that regard, he carried John Daly's golf bag in the Missouri State Championship golf tournament during the summer of 1983.

After completing a killer year of scholastic golf as a junior, Daly was feeling invincible as he went into the state amateur tournament. The Helias team had won the state championship in their division and had compiled a 66–9 record overall. Daly had a season average of one over par for 243 competitive holes of golf. He also held every record the school kept in golf, including a score of five under for nine holes and the season low average.

In the state amateur championship that summer, Daly wasn't playing against high school kids anymore. The tournament was open to all ages. Nonetheless, Daly made it to the final round, where he was paired with a highly ranked college player from Kansas City. The college kid from the big city could barely conceal his contempt for these high schoolers from Jefferson City—the roly-poly boy golfer and his buffed-out fullback of a caddie. He was certain this was going to be over fast.

As is so often the case in golf, however, appearances were deceiving. Regardless of his other shortcomings and disabilities in life, John Daly could play golf by now—and he knew it. When he was swinging well and every shot came easily, he had the self-confidence of a man holding the only weapon in a street fight.

Every time he hit a good shot that day, and there were many, he would turn to Chris Hentges and say: "I am unstoppable. No one can touch me." He would walk up to hairy, twenty-foot putts and, barely studying the break, would say: "This is going to fall." Almost always, it did.

As the match and the demonstration of golfing skills progressed, the college kid was speechless. He could only shake his head in amazement. Playing his best, he was at two under after thirteen holes. Daly was eight under and about to become the state amateur champion at seventeen.

All his feelings of mastery on the golf course disappeared when Daly walked off the eighteenth green. He went right back to thinking of himself as an ugly—and now fat—country boy from Arkansas, and nobody seemed to be able to help him with that. This caused him to be shy, and he was so displeased by his appearance that he avoided cameras whenever possible.

Later that summer, he and Chris Hentges were fooling around with a football in a lot next to the Dalys' house. In addition to playing fullback, Hentges was the kicker and punter for his father's team, yet he discovered that day that Daly could propel the ball farther with his foot than Hentges could.

Hentges was considerably more muscular than Daly, but watching him in action, Hentges realized that, as with golf, most of Daly's ability to strike the ball explosively derived from his extraordinary timing. He had the natural ability to coordinate all of his muscle movements in perfect harmony so that the resulting swing, or kick, was more than the sum of its parts.

Hentges didn't know that Daly had advanced twice to the national semifinals of an annual punt, pass, and kick competition that was sponsored by the National Football League. Daly had left that behind when he was nine because he didn't want to get hurt and endanger his golfing career.

When he saw how Daly could kick, Chris Hentges began a heavy lobbying campaign to get John to join the football team, which had done well the year before and was expected to improve in the upcoming year. John was straight with him, telling him he just didn't want to risk injury. Chris said that wasn't a problem, as he was on good terms with the coach, and they could work a deal. John would become the Crusaders' kicker, but he wouldn't have to tackle or block anyone. Just as in the pros, Daly could hang back out of the action after his kicks.

That fall's football team was one of the finest Helias High School ever had. Chris Hentges set a school record for most yards gained in a game, 306, in a lopsided contest in which the Crusaders scored ten touchdowns. Daly kicked nine points-after-touchdowns and was about to kick his tenth when the clock ran out. Ray Hentges was so pleased with Daly's performance that he gave Daly unofficial credit for the tenth kick. The team, which had gone 6–3 the previous year, was undefeated through the early part of the season.

If there was a sore point on the team amid all the jubilation about the winning streak, it was over John Daly's status as the only noncombatant member of the football team. When the rest of the team went swooping down the field after the guy returning a kickoff, Daly fell back from the fray, trying to look inconspicuous. Since he had gained nearly sixty pounds in the last year and a half, that was almost impossible.

Daly, who had been boyishly slender when he arrived in Jefferson City, weighed 220 pounds as a senior—and a good bit of that was fat. When he cinched up the belt on his hip pads and shimmied into a tight pair of football pants, the results weren't flattering. All of his extra weight was displaced toward his waist, where it formed a most conspicuous roll of flesh that kept trying to escape from the confines of his jersey.

The guys on the team started kidding John good-naturedly about his aversion to tackling and about his weight. Given the cruelty that children can sometimes manifest toward those who vary from the norm, it was relatively minor stuff. Still, it bothered Daly, who was especially sensitive to criticism.

These issues all came to the forefront late in the football season, when the undefeated Helias Crusaders took on their rivals from Rock Bridge High School. It was a hard-fought defensive contest from the start, and even Chris Hentges couldn't move the ball. Helias managed to post a 6–0 lead as a result of two field goals that were kicked by John Daly.

That slim lead, and Helias's unblemished record, seemed secure until late in the game, when a crafty running back from Rock Bridge grabbed a Daly kickoff and started up the field. Helias players leaped, scrambled, and lunged for the boy, but he shook them all off. In a flash, he had virtually a clear field. The only thing between him and the goal line was one opposing player: John Daly. The only Helias player who could save the game hadn't tackled a single opponent during the entire season.

Daly drew a bead on the runner as he closed in. But as the moment of contact neared, Daly couldn't recall that he was supposed to wrap his arms around someone when he tackled him. Instead, Daly plastered his arms to his side and dove headfirst, like a human torpedo, at the other player's feet.

The kid returning the ball was so disconcerted that, although Daly never actually touched him, he tripped over Daly as he lay there. This sent the runner careening through the air, before he crashed to the ground. Daly had saved the game.

Daly's unorthodox tackle, combined with his two field goals, made him the unquestioned hero of the game—at least to his teammates. The Rock Bridge High School coach was not amused by the bizarre style of his defeat. When he was approached by a reporter from a Columbus, Missouri, newspaper after the game, he voiced his disapproval. His team, the Rock Bridge coach said, had just been defeated by "the Pillsbury Dough Boy in pads."

When the quote appeared in the newspaper the next day, Daly, who was already tremendously self-conscious about his appearance, was devastated. Then the worst possible thing happened: Kids at school picked up on the quote and turned it into a nickname. Soon Daly couldn't even walk down the halls between classes without someone calling out, "Hey, Dough Boy."

The football team went on to a 10–0 season, and the golf team was virtually guaranteed another state championship come spring, but John Daly didn't seem to be relishing these prospects. He began disengaging from his friends and spending more time by himself, and everybody guessed what was happening.

All fall Daly had been hinting around that he might have to go back to Arkansas soon. He had been clear all along that he wanted to play college golf at the University of Arkansas, even though there were plenty of schools in Missouri that would have loved to have him. Then one day in March he walked up to Chris Hentges in the lunchroom and said he was leaving—that it was out of his hands.

Daly had been offered a golf scholarship at the University of Arkansas, but it was limited to the lower tuition paid by Arkansas residents. If he could get back to Arkansas in time to graduate from a high school there, he'd be considered a state resident, and he could save his folks some money.

Finding a place to stay wouldn't be a problem, as the family had held on to their house in Dardanelle as a retirement and vacation home. But Jim Daly's work was keeping him on the road again, and he and Lou couldn't move down to Arkansas. So John and his brother, James, who had learned to party so well in Jefferson City, were sent back to Dardanelle to set up house by themselves.

3

Salad Days

The sun was warm and the sky clear when the Daly boys rolled back into Dardanelle in March. It was the time of year when high school seniors often become infected with a particularly virulent strain of spring fever, and John Daly was no exception. With the arrival of good weather there were a lot of things he wanted to do, but going to school wasn't one of them.

He had already been awarded a sports scholarship to college, making the last three months of his senior year a sham. He didn't know that many kids at Dardanelle High School, and his parents weren't around. His brother, James—who was known as Jamie in these parts—had finished his schooling at Helias the year before. He was contemplating a career as a bricklayer, but he was also adept at forging absence notes.

John didn't spend a lot of time confined at Dardanelle High School. When the educators there were kind enough to award him a diploma anyway, he told them to stick it in the mail, as he'd be skipping graduation to play in a golf tournament out of state.

John spent much of his time at the Bay Ridge Boat and Golf Club, where the locals had seen bits and pieces of his game during summer visits to his old hometown. Daly was already something of a legend there, and when he returned this time, the members brought him to the attention of Rick Ross, who was giving lessons at the club and helping coach the golf team up the road at Arkansas Tech in Russellville.

Ross had been told that Daly could hit the ball as far as Ross himself could, even though Ross was ten years older and an accomplished enough golfer to be contemplating a run at the PGA Tour. When the two finally met on the driving range, Ross watched Daly hit some balls and was highly impressed.

"You're obviously a good player with great hands," Ross said. "The sense of feel in your swing is more than I've ever seen, and I've played with pros. Are you thinking about pursuing this?"

Daly scoffed at him. "I'm going to be playing the tour," he said.

Ross smiled. He had expected Daly to say that he wanted to give it a try, not that there simply weren't any other options in his life. He liked the kid's determination, but he suspected that Daly didn't have the faintest understanding of how difficult it was going to be—of the obstacles life was going to throw at him, and the ones that he could create for himself.

Having lost his father at sixteen, Ross knew what it was to have a dream but to be lacking in direction. He had wanted to attend college right after high school and work on his golf game, but he didn't want to be a financial burden on his widowed mother. He joined the Navy instead, serving six years on submarines, then came back and earned a math degree with the government's help. His golf was still sharp enough that he kept thinking about trying to get on the tour, but he also had a wife and wanted to start a family. He understood firsthand how complicated life could get.

21

After Daly had hit some solid drives that day, Ross decided to give this impetuous young man his first lesson. He asked if he could try out Daly's driver. When Daly passed it over, Ross blew some balls down to the far end of the driving range, fifteen to twenty yards past Daly. Daly looked over with fire in his eyes and asked for his driver back. He banged balls for another hour, trying unsuccessfully to outdrive Ross.

Daly and Ross became good friends after that, as Ross helped Daly improve his game. Both of them were largely self-taught golfers who had modeled their swings on that of Jack Nicklaus, although it was Daly who had Nicklaus's killer instincts. They played a lot of golf that summer, and every time they did, Daly tried to outdo Ross in any aspect of the game he could.

Shooting low score was never enough. Daly wanted to drive it farther, he wanted to knock his second shot closer to the pin, he wanted to record more birdies. When he wasn't swinging out of his shoes to find another way to add a couple more inches to his drives, he was devising new ways to measure himself against other guys on the golf course—and in life.

He saw golf as he did everything else, from the quantity of alcohol he could drink to how fast he could drive a car—it was all a test of John Daly against the rest of the world. By winning any of these little contests, he could momentarily feel less bad about himself. It also helped him perpetuate in his own mind the myth that he really could bend the world to his will.

Ross tried to counsel Daly about these things, but it didn't work. Daly would simply climb further into himself. They'd sometime have pointed disagreements and Daly's volatile temper would approach the boiling point, but he wouldn't vent it or release it. At these times Ross would tell Daly to hit him, to get it out, because he was going to kill himself keeping it bottled up, but Daly wouldn't do it. He'd much rather beat on himself and take himself down than let it go.

So Rick Ross concentrated on helping Daly with his game and on being a friend to him. He recognized early on that Daly's personality was such that you couldn't force him into anything. He had to reach a conclusion himself before he could do anything about a situation—no matter how minute the problem or decision was.

After a summer of easy pleasures in Dardanelle, Daly went off to Fayetteville and the University of Arkansas, 120 miles away in the far northwestern corner of the state. He had added the trophy from the Arkansas state amateur tournament to his cache that summer—to complement the previous year's state title from Missouri—while appending even more heft to his five-foot-eleven-inch frame. By the time he flopped on the bed in his dorm room for the first time in late August, Daly weighed a massive 235 pounds. The people who gave out the scholarships at the university were not pleased about this.

Steve Loy had been hired as the golf coach at the University of Arkansas the previous summer by Frank Broyles, the legendary Arkansas football coach turned athletic director, who had transformed the formerly obscure school into a national football power in the 1960s. In a state without professional sports teams to cheer for and rally around, and with few national figures offering reflected glory by calling Arkansas home, Broyles's dynasty-building turned Arkansas Razorback football into the new state religion. The spirits of a goodly percentage of the people in Arkansas—not to mention the cash contributions of tens of thousands of university alumni—alternately soared or plummeted according to the performance of Frank Broyles's teams. He would be called Coach Broyles for life, the way a man of the cloth would always be referred to as Father or Bishop.

When Broyles announced his retirement as football coach in 1976, it was the most shocking news to hit Arkansas since word arrived about the outcome of the Civil War. But there was an upside to this story. Coach Broyles would be staying on as athletic director, and he intended to use that position to do for other Arkansas sports programs what he had already done for football.

The school's golf teams had never accomplished anything in divisional competitions, traditionally finishing in the bottom half of their conference. With the coffers filled with the contributions of grateful alumni, Broyles meant to change that. He went looking for a new golf coach who could shake things up.

Broyles found Steve Loy at Scottsdale Community College in Arizona. After an extended stint heading up the football program there, Loy had coached golf for six years and compiled an impressive record. His teams had won National Junior College Athletic Association championships in 1982 and 1983.

Loy had done very well for himself at a two-year college in the desert, where he was a relaxed and easygoing man who was the master of all the cacti he surveyed. When he accepted Broyles's offer to move up to a four-year college that was also a big-time, big-money sports school, it was a Faustian deal at best. It was a tremendous career opportunity, but if Loy didn't produce, he would discover that disapproval could be expressed in ways that would give him the night sweats.

The formerly even-tempered Loy suddenly decided he'd better coach golf the way generals run armies. Every day during the season, student golfers would report to the practice tee at 1500 hours. They would work on their short game for 120 minutes, then move out and perform drills on the course. Only when these exercises were completed would the golfers be permitted to play a practice round.

During tournaments, Loy would instruct his players on how to play specific holes, down to what club they were to use. They could shoot only high-percentage shots and were never allowed to gamble and shoot for the pin. During a Southwest Conference tournament, when his players came to a 190-yard par three, he ordered them to lay up short of the green because it had too many bunkers around it.

Off the course, there was an evening curfew, mandatory class attendance, regular physical conditioning programs, and matching red blazers for everyone to wear when the team went on the road. Loy did give his players one option: They could either follow his orders to the letter, or they could cease to exist on the golf team.

This formula worked well enough for Loy to be voted Southwest Conference coach of the year after his first season at Arkansas. Then all 235 pounds of John Daly—his most promising recruit!—waddled into Loy's office, and the coach felt his shorts creep up.

Even though Loy considered Daly to be one of the most naturally talented golfers he had ever seen, he decided on the spot that the boy was going to require massive intervention. As far as Loy was concerned, if a player wasn't physically fit, he couldn't be mentally fit, and thus could never succeed at perhaps the most mentally challenging sport of all. This Daly boy, Loy decided, needed a discipline program that would stop just short of the whip.

Loy called Jim and Lou Daly in and outlined a diet and exercise regime designed to reconfigure their son. It was heavy on salads and mostly absent everything else. As a short-term incentive, Loy prohibited John from playing competitive golf until he shed some of the bulk. He would also be subjected to more weigh-ins than a Weight Watchers convention-eer, and if Daly relapsed and gained a pound, he would be running laps until he puked.

As a first-semester freshman, Daly was a shy, immature, sensitive, and scared kid who suddenly found himself adrift on the sprawling campus of a massive university. It was Jefferson City High School on steroids. Being disoriented for a few weeks was only to be expected, but having to face the loss of golf was devastating.

In a life in which John Daly thought he did many things worse than most people, golf was what he believed—for good reason—that he did better than practically everyone else. Depriving him of this would be like burning off his fingerprints. If ever there was a situation designed to foster overreaction in a young man hardwired for excess, here it was.

Daly immediately abandoned Loy's weight-loss program and devised a special liquid-and-smoke diet of his own. It was composed of equal parts Marlboros, diet Coke, black coffee, and Jack Daniel's. Daly made the transition from beer to his father's whisky after someone ludicrously convinced him that the hard stuff was less caloric than beer. As for solid food, Daly passed on that.

For three miserable months, Daly followed Loy around like a neglected puppy in search of a head rubbing, all the while holding to his routine of stimulants and depressants—caffeine in the morning to bring him up, alcohol to crash at night. In less than ninety days, Daly had distilled off sixty-five pounds of fat through the miracle of chemistry. He started eating food again then, but he also maintained his warm, ongoing, never-let-you-down relationship with Uncle Jack Daniel's.

The guys from the golf team all roomed, hung out, and cursed Steve Loy together, and being eighteen to twenty-two years old, none of them thought too much about Daly's drinking at first. Hell, everybody was doing it. You had a bunch of guys at their sexual peak, away from home for the first time, with all these delicious girls around. And they were varsity athletes at a school where jocks reigned. Of course they were going to drink. You went out and met girls and got drunk. For horny young guys, it was the unabridged definition of fun. This was especially true for Daly, who was now svelte for the first time since tenth grade.

Even though he was five foot eleven, Daly had always thought of himself as short, fat, and ugly. He believed that no woman would find him attractive or want to be sexual with him unless she was drunk. Then he could do okay sometimes, and that was a pretty good deal.

Now that he was slim, all of a sudden girls really liked Daly. And, my God, after that long barren period, did he love them in return! The second a woman showed any interest in him, Daly fell so irrevocably in love with her that it was as though he were trying to turn his life into a walking, talking tearjerker of a country ballad. He even dated a woman named Scarlett. The new attention from women was wonderful, but rather than risk finding out if it was really him that they liked, he kept a supply of booze close at hand to keep things cordial.

Daly's roommate, chief partying companion, and teammate at school was Petey King, a lean and angular six-foot-three-inch freshman from North Little Rock whose father covered Arkansas sports for the Associated Press. At first King never paid that much attention to Daly's drinking when they were out, since he was drinking, too. Then he began to notice that Daly kept on drinking long after everyone else had quit for the night. There just didn't seem to be any stopping him once he got going.

King was still a teenager, and he didn't know what it meant to be an alcoholic, but he thought that there was a fine line there and he was pretty sure Daly was going over it on occasion. Sometimes that would result in funny things happening, such as the time they stayed out too late, drank too much, and decided to ditch classes the next morning.

The drill was that whenever anyone was sleeping in, they

first made sure all the doors were locked, since Steve Loy sent an assistant coach around each morning to do a bed check. On this morning, however, the golf team members in the adjoining suite had forgotten to lock the door to the bathroom they shared. The assistant came in through the bathroom, discovered Daly and King still in bed, and ran to get Loy, who came back and exploded in rage.

Daly and King paid for that evening by being subjected to one of Loy's favorite forms of punishment. They were made to run continuous laps through the streets of Fayetteville without stopping—a provision Loy enforced by driving behind them and observing from the comfort of his car.

Because no one knew any better, the golf team got used to Daly's drinking, dismissing it with "Oh, he's drunk again." Sometimes when he was especially drunk, he would get mean and destructive and start knocking over and breaking stuff in one of the dorm rooms, and the guys would calm him down. But the situation got catastrophic when Daly started drinking himself into unconsciousness.

The first time he drank until he vomited and passed out, Daly's teammates were terrified. They slapped his face and shook him, but he didn't respond at all. He just lay on the floor looking ashen and dead. No one knew what was going on— whether he was really dying or what. They were just a bunch of college kids, and nothing in their lives had prepared them for this.

They quickly decided that this was a very dangerous situation and that they had to get Daly immediate medical attention. They picked him up, carried him out to a car, stuffed him in, and tore to the hospital. What happened there wasn't a pleasant sight, as medical personnel snaked a tube down Daly's throat and sucked out the contents of his stomach.

The guys from the golf team waited in the lobby until Daly was revived and the doctors said he was going to be okay.

Some of them tried to talk to him about it afterward, and so did Steve Loy when he discovered what had transpired. Those words of concern made absolutely no difference. John Daly would be admitted to the hospital in alcohol-induced stupors twice more before he left the University of Arkansas—and then he would try to drink himself to death twice more again after that.

If Daly wasn't getting into trouble for his drinking that difficult freshman year, his temper would be causing him problems. Once, in a qualifying round to determine who would get to travel to a tournament, Daly hit a poor shot out of a bunker, diminishing the chance that he would make the cut. He threw his sand wedge at his golf bag in disgust.

Seeing this, and wanting to teach Daly a lesson, Steve Loy came over, picked up the wedge, and smacked Daly on the ankle with it, knocking him to the ground. When Daly could stand, he got up and walked off the golf course without saying a word. He didn't come back to practice for a week.

Other times he would get mad at his performance on the course and seem to go into a trance, with God only knows what running through his mind. He wouldn't say a word and would look straight ahead. He would hit his ball and take off chasing after it before anyone else had hit. When he got to the green, he would hit his putt and, seeing that it was going to go in, walk after it so quickly that he would almost beat his ball to the hole. He'd keep this up until his anger at himself subsided and he rejoined the human race.

Steve Loy didn't let John Daly play in many tournaments his freshman year, but by his sophomore year Daly had three top-ten finishes, including a fourth-place finish in the Southwest Conference tournament. At the National College Athletic Association tournament, he shot a course-record round of 65 on the way to finishing fourteenth.

More importantly, outside of college golf, Daly was scoring

some impressive accomplishments, even though he had just turned twenty. After playing consistently in local and sectional qualifying tournaments, he earned a spot to compete as an amateur in the U.S. Open—one of the four major tournaments of professional golf. For the first time in his life, John Daly would be teeing it up with the big boys.

In 1986 the Open was being held at Shinnecock Hills Golf Club in Southampton, New York. The golf club was one of the oldest and most prestigious in the United States, and it was located in the vicinity of a string of chic Long Island beach towns that were the summer playground of Manhattan's moneyed and socially connected elite. No one was ever going to confuse Shinnecock with the Bay Ridge Boat and Golf Club, or the Hamptons with Lake Dardanelle.

Daly wandered around the posh surroundings as carefully as a boy with squeaky shoes trying to sneak out of church. In his mind, the list of really stupid and embarrassing things he could do to make a fool of himself stretched all the way back to Arkansas. Everything was going fine until one day, here was Daly on the driving range, and who comes walking by but Jack Nicklaus.

After all those years of mooning after him on TV and studying his swing, there is Jack Nicklaus—who at age forty-six had just won his twentieth major tournament—a couple of feet away. Nicklaus looks right at John Daly and says hi, really nice and pleasant, as though Daly was a new neighbor or something.

So what does John Daly do after all these years of waiting and planning and hoping for this moment to occur? He does nothing. He stands there frozen, with his eyes bulging out and his jaw locked shut, and watches Jack Nicklaus walk right past him. Then he realized that, like a fool, not only had he not said hi back, he'd also let Jack get away without asking him for his autograph.

It didn't occur to Daly that he had earned his way into this most prestigious of tournaments, and that at this very moment, he and Nicklaus were equals of sorts. They were both inside the ropes. Daly could walk over to him any time he wanted. They could have a conversation. But he couldn't bring himself to do it. He was sure he'd only say something dumb. Instead, Daly moved back out of the way and watched Jack swing.

He couldn't get over how methodical Jack was. Nicklaus went through the same preswing routine on the practice range that he used on the course. Everything was so precise, so slow and deliberate. When Daly was on the course, he was taking three looks, three waggles, then *bam*—he was hitting the ball and moving on.

On Thursday Daly's tee time was at the end of the day, where the unknowns get stuck. It had been raining all day, and the wind was blowing in good off the Atlantic Ocean. Daly made it to the fourth hole before he stumbled. He hooked a ball way the hell over into the rough. All the marshals who help you look for your ball were inside for cocktail hour. He wrote the ball off and dropped another. Then he lost that in the rough, too.

Right there he wanted to quit. What was the point? He couldn't win now. And if Daly couldn't win, he wasn't really interested in playing. But all the papers back home had been writing about how Daly was the first Arkansan in all these years to play in a U.S. Open, so he kept going. Then when he called in to the *Arkansas Gazette* that night, he said, "I just hope I didn't let the state down. I'm glad I stayed with it and never gave up. I think I got a lot of respect from a lot of people by not giving up. . . . I just want the state to know I tried up here and never gave up."

Daly almost died the next morning on the first tee when the sign bearer came out with the sign showing him to be eighteen over par. But the sun broke through the clouds that day, and John Daly came back and shot a 76 at the U.S. Open. He still missed the cut by fourteen shots, but somehow he managed to understand that this wasn't so bad for a twenty-year-old, and that if he kept at it, he would have another chance someday.

4

The Road to Blytheville

Steve Loy was offered a job coaching golf at Arizona State University starting in the spring semester of 1987, and he took it. John Daly was faced with a coaching change in the middle of his junior year, and it was a drastic one. Bill Woodley, the incoming coach, was as dissimilar from Loy as any two men could be and still share an occupation.

To Loy, coaching was essentially regimentation and a striving for idealized norms. He believed there was one correct way to play golf, and he measured his team members against that. Woodley, who had been coaching at Texas Christian University, thought it was entirely individualistic and subjective. If something worked for a player, that was good enough for him. Loy would line guys up and have them hit seven-irons simultaneously for hours, while Woodley would tell his boys to decide for themselves what part of their game needed work.

Initially the guys on the golf team thought Daly would benefit most from this radical change of approach. All his instincts were attuned to playing wide-open golf. He wanted to swing as hard as possible off the tee, and then he wanted to hit his second shot at the flag. If he got in trouble this way, so what? He would scramble and deal with it. Steve Loy lived to protect against the downside. He'd strongly disapproved of the way Daly tried to play golf, and he'd let him know that frequently and vociferously.

Bill Woodley was perfectly amenable to Daly's playing however he wanted, and for a while it looked like a perfect combination. Daly was leading his version of the good life: drinking as much as ever, smoking heavily, attending class infrequently, and playing a lot of golf. When he did show up for a test in one of his classes, he would sometimes sign his name at the top of the page and leave—which didn't win Daly or the golf program any friends among the academic faculty.

While Woodley cut Daly a lot of slack on the golf course, his disapproval of Daly's off-course behavior came to know no limits—especially after Daly had to be taken to the hospital again for an episode of alcohol poisoning a month into Woodley's watch. The coach ordered Daly into alcoholism counseling, but Daly attended only a few sessions and then stopped, saying he didn't need any help with his drinking. But the coach, an avid hunter who filled his office with stuffed and mounted prey, wasn't giving up that easily.

Woodley had experienced alcoholism in people close to him, and he knew that alcoholics often bullied everyone who let them get away with it. Although alcoholism is a disease, the self-indulgence, predictability, and sheer tediousness of a drunk is maddening when dealt with regularly. One approach to attempting to change this behavior is to confront the alcoholic and to be absolutely steadfast about it. This was the path that Woodley chose to follow with Daly. Given that Daly was playing well for the golf team, and that—miraculously—his drinking never affected his golf, it was a calculated risk.

Woodley wrote to Daly in May offering him a scholarship for his senior year, but he included the proviso that the free ride, and Daly's position on the golf team, were dependent upon him giving up drinking and smoking—although Woodley himself enjoyed a good chew—and on Daly attending classes regularly, just like everyone else.

From the day he had arrived in Fayetteville, it had been Daly's intention to graduate from the University of Arkansas. This had nothing to do with acquiring an education. Daly hadn't read much beyond *Sports Illustrated* or *Golf Digest* since freshman orientation. Rather, becoming a Razorback and picking up a degree of some sort was a rite of passage for anyone who lived in the state and dreamed of greater glories. Having an Arkansas diploma conferred on you meant you never had to look back.

But now, here was this son of a bitch Woodley trying to tell John Daly how to live his life, saying that he had to stop drinking and smoking, and start going to class—like any of them had anything to do with playing golf. As if Woodley was going to threaten John Daly and order him around and get away with it.

At about this time, Rick Ross, Daly's friend and teacher in Dardanelle, had returned from a not fully successful attempt to raise a family and make a living playing on the PGA Tour, and they had been talking a lot about whether John was ready to turn pro.

Daly had been making the trek over the Ozarks and down I–40 to Dardanelle more weekends than not since freshman year. When Ross gave up on the tour, he took a job as a teaching pro at Rosswood Country Club in Pine Bluff, and Daly came there. The club was closed on Mondays, and John would head down on Sunday night and stay over and they would practice on the course on Monday, hitting balls until their hands ached.

Ross didn't think hitting balls well was going to be Daly's problem with going on the PGA Tour. Ross knew how hard it was to make your weekly expenses when you were undercapitalized to begin with, and how lucky you had to be to make everything work when you needed it to. As anybody who had ever tried to play the tour was well aware, there seemed to be an endless supply of talented golfers with the same dreams.

None of that mattered to Daly. His mantra was that he was not afraid of playing anyone. He was an aggressive player, and he thought courageousness was all it took to win. He had won state amateur tournaments as a teenager, and he was ready to get on with becoming one of the best golfers who had ever walked the earth. His goals and expectations were exalted and unshakable. It was the ingenuous braggadocio of someone who had spent a lot of time creating big ripples in small ponds.

Daly would learn that the precariousness of life on the tour began with the PGA Qualifying Tournament, where forty to fifty players earn the right to play in sanctioned events during the following year. More than seven hundred men spend several thousand dollars each to enter this annual tournament; fewer than two hundred survive even the first stage. Those who carry on are subjected to a final six-round, 108-hole marathon. Everyone else gets to sit out another year, and those who make the tour but fail to finish in the top 125 on the earnings list have to come back to join them at next year's qualifying tournament.

Few players win their playing privileges the first time out, and Ross was counseling Daly to be psychologically prepared to go through four qualifying tournaments until he got on—and stayed on—the PGA Tour. Daly insisted he could handle that, but Ross wasn't so sure. He was especially worried about Daly's volatile personality, which at the moment was driving him to quit college as a way of thumbing his nose at Bill Woodley.

When Daly decided to leave school, he made sure Woodley

learned of it in an appropriately in-your-face way. That summer Daly told everybody but Woodley that he was quitting Arkansas and turning pro. Woodley discovered that his attempt to shock Daly into sobriety had failed when a reporter called in late July—a month before school started—and asked for Woodley's reaction to Daly's announcement. Woodley, who now had a huge hole in the golf team and a scholarship that it was too late to use, managed to get a "no comment" out, but he was furious.

Meanwhile Daly had been off playing in amateur tournaments in the area that summer, and one of them took him to Blytheville, a farming town of 22,500 people in the Mississippi Delta lands of northeastern Arkansas. Cotton was still king there, and although much of the farming was mechanized, little else seemed to have changed from earlier times.

The Blytheville Country Club, with its flat, tree-lined fairways, was out on the far reaches of Highway 61 North, near a small and unselfconscious cluster of fancy houses. There was no high land for these houses to occupy, but they were situated away from the dusty fields and the used car lot downtown, where vehicle prices were noted on the windshields in sums payable weekly.

The Missouri border was close enough that you could ride a mule there if you had to, so when the townspeople wanted a motto for their village, they thought about how near the Northerners—and all of their abruptness—were. Then they had some signs made up: Blytheville, Where Southern Hospitality Begins.

A man playing golf in the summer sun and cloaking humidity in this part of the world could work up a thirst, and so it was that one night after the Blytheville tournament John Daly found himself in the bar of the Holiday Inn on Main Street. The Holiday Inn was the class hostelry in town, the place where they'd lay out a copious buffet for early Sunday supper, and folks would wear their good shoes and bring their out-of-town kin and everybody would act a little bit constrained.

In the bar, John Daly saw a woman with a spiked haircut that drifted between blond and brunette, and when he asked, she said her name was Dale Crafton. She was a few years older than he; her family owned land and crops in these parts, and had for some time. Her grandmother, Ethelyn Dunlap, had been the state champion of the Arkansas Senior Women's Golf Association. None of this mattered overly much to Daly. It was more important that she seemed to like him. He was already falling in love.

As they got to know each other, she began accompanying him to tournaments he played in that summer. Before anyone knew what to make of it, they were getting married. He was twenty-one, and a woman who was refined enough to send handwritten thank-you notes to her friends loved him. That had never happened to him before, and he wasn't sure it would again. He wanted to please her and make her happy. They had an elaborate wedding in Blytheville. John would have been satisfied with bringing a preacher in, then having everybody go over to the hamburger place for double cheeseburgers, but a showy affair was what Dale wanted, so he went along.

John took Dale up to Jefferson City to meet Ray Hentges, his old golf coach at Helias High School, then John went on to play in the Missouri Open at the Country Club of Missouri, in Columbus. It was his first tournament as a professional golfer, and his performance was just as he had presumed all of these years. He shot an opening round of 65, slipped to 73 in the wind, and came charging back with a 66 in the final round to win the tournament by four strokes. His first golf paycheck was $6,000.

The following week he went to the municipal course at

Burns Park in North Little Rock and finished second in the Arkansas Open. The week after that he finished second in the Elks Invitational in Duncan, Oklahoma, where he earned $2,500. At the end of his first six weeks as a professional golfer, Daly had won $17,000.

Sheeeeee-it. Here was everybody talking all these years about how hard it was to make it as a professional golfer. Here he had wasted all this time. In a month and a half he had earned more than many people in Arkansas would make during all of 1987—and he was playing nickel-and-dime state tournaments. Wait until the kid got on the PGA Tour, where many tournaments had $1 million purses.

Filled with self-assurance, Daly took some of his winnings and registered for the PGA Tour Qualifying Tournament. Sure enough, he breezed through the first round. The second tournament, outside of Houston, was tougher, but he still made the cut by two strokes. Then it was off to Palm Coast, Florida, for the finals. Like a gambler who was letting it ride, this was strictly all-or-nothing. It also involved a measure of luck. Unfortunately, Daly crashed and missed the cut. He wandered off the course with 129 other guys who were hurting too much to draw a deep breath. Most of the pro golf they would be playing for the next year would be sporadic and low-rent.

John and Dale were living in Little Rock at this time, but Dale was getting on his case because she wanted to move to Blytheville. Her family and friends were there, and it was closer to Memphis, Tennessee, where she sometimes worked as a hand model. Besides, her family was offering them a house to live in for free.

John Daly had never wanted anybody to give him anything, but he went along and moved to Blytheville just the same. It made him feel like a cheapskate, though, to be living in a house he wasn't paying for. And with it being her money and her town, he felt as if there were a crowd in residence: John, Dale, and her family.

With John having missed the cut for the PGA Tour, he wasn't going to be making the money he had planned—at least not right away. As far as he was concerned, he thought they should be living within their means. Instead, he found himself living according to the standards, and with some of the same money, that Dale had been used to when she was with her family.

Almost from the beginning, Dale and John were on different paths. She wanted to settle down and be comfortable, and she was used to accepting things from her family. John wanted to go off and conquer the world, and he thought taking things from other people implied weakness and need—feelings he was extremely uncomfortable with. He had never learned that sharing could be an expression of love.

Regardless of where they were living, John was going to be stuck doing low-budget travel to small-time tournaments until he made it to the PGA Tour. That could easily last for three or four years, and the style and amount of that travel became another topic of controversy between him and Dale.

Sometimes John would tell friends that Dale wanted to travel with him but that he couldn't afford to bring her along, so he wanted her to stay home with her family. Other times he would say she didn't want to travel at all or didn't want to rough it on the road to the extent that he did.

John did travel, though, sometimes with Dale along, but with nothing resembling the fairy-tale success he enjoyed during the first six weeks of his pro career. He struggled and missed cuts and drove long distances home with nothing but a bit more experience to show for his efforts. It was part of the normal learning curve of becoming a professional golfer. But to a kid who had won the Missouri amateur championship at seventeen, it was a bitter dose of reality—one he relied on Jack

Daniel's to make more sufferable. Almost from the beginning, John's perpetual drinking was an additional point of contention in his fragile marriage.

The Dalys and the Craftons both knew John and Dale were having problems getting along and that they were arguing, but everyone hoped things would straighten out when John got his career and all of its enormous promise going. During 1988, however, that day sometimes seemed eons away. John entered the PGA Tour Qualifying Tournament that fall, but once again he was eliminated in the final round. It was crushing, both financially and emotionally. At least this year he had an alternative.

Steve Loy had recruited a number of South African golfers when he was at the University of Arkansas, and Daly had learned about the South African professional golf tour from them. Called the Sunshine Tour, it ran during the southern hemisphere's summer, from December to February. When Daly failed to make the PGA Tour at the end of 1988, he decided to see if he could find sponsors who would stake him front money for an attempt at golf at the bottom of the world.

He managed to sell twelve $1,000 shares in himself, with the understanding that after his expenses were deducted, all of the shareholders would split Daly's winnings with him on his return. Such sponsorships are a common arrangement that young golfers make, usually with people who are more interested in helping their careers develop than in realizing huge returns.

While Daly was heading for South Africa, there were similar overseas tours in Asia and Europe that young American golfers went to in order to hone their skills and learn how to win against intense competition. Daly opted to go to South Africa for two reasons: he had University of Arkansas contacts there, and since English was the common language, it was a great place to learn how to deal with the media. If you went to

Asia, you didn't get interviewed. In South Africa Daly might be able to get on TV, and that appealed to him.

Daly appeared in Durban, South Africa, the first week in January in an attempt to qualify for the Dewar's White Label tournament. There were forty-one other Americans there with the same idea, but Daly beat them all to finish tied for fourth in his maiden outing. Two weeks later he tied for fourth again, then tied for eleventh place in two events.

In February southern Africa was hit with persistent rainstorms that thoroughly saturated every golf course on the Sunshine Tour calendar. The entire first day of the Swazi Sun Classic was washed out, and the tournament was shortened to three days. When play resumed, John Daly responded to the soggy conditions as though he were part waterfowl. The wet fairways tamed his wild shots and prevented the ball from bounding into the rough, improving his lie. He shot two 67's and a 69 at the Royal Swazi Golf Club in Swaziland, missing a twelve-foot putt on the final hole that would have sent the tournament into a playoff. Nonetheless, a tie for second place wasn't bad for a twenty-two-year-old who was far more than a hog call from home.

He missed only one cut that season, although he got food poisoning and had to withdraw from the Palabora Classic. He won over $23,000, plus something else that was beyond monetary value. Every week, eight to ten thousand spectators attended tournaments on the Sunshine Tour and cheered for the top contenders. On three occasions in 1989, that lofty company included John Daly. It was the first time he had ever played well enough in a professional tournament to have strangers follow him around the course and voice their approval. It was a transforming experience for him.

After a lifetime spent alternately beating himself up psychologically or abusing himself physically, Daly suddenly found himself the recipient of spontaneous applause from thousands of people who cared about only his golf. They clapped in appreciation of his talent, and because his performance entertained them. Such a warm and unbiased reception was enough to make a man wonder if he might not be worth something after all.

John Daly returned to the United States exuding newfound confidence in his golf game but still firmly in touch with his Arkansas roots. South Africa had been two terrific months, but the next PGA Tour qualifying tournament was the better part of a year away. A guy needed to made a living—especially if he was married and wanted to support his wife.

Daly rang up the *Arkansas Gazette* to report his good fortunes in Africa, but also to do a little promotional work. Over the last few years, Daly had built a putting green at the back of his parents' house in Dardanelle and then moved on to create a sizable driving range, complete with lights, down the hill from their home. Jim Daly was the manager of the range, and until recently it had been a place where local folks could come by and whale the bejesus out of a bucket of golf balls after they finished their shift at the Tyson chicken plant in town.

Now Dardanelle's most widely traveled resident, and only professional golfer, wanted folks to know that he was available to give golf lessons at the Wildcat Hollow Driving Range. He gave his dad's home phone number so people could call for an appointment. Dale Daly might well have wondered how John expected to handle the logistics of this, as she thought they were living in Blytheville, 250 miles away.

Daly continued to work slavishly at his career, and by hustling his way through a series of qualifying tournaments, he earned a berth in the U.S. Open for the second time, and the first time as a professional. He broke another barrier when he made the two-day cut at the tournament in June 1989 at the Oak Hill Country Club in Rochester, New York, shooting 74, then 67. In addition to being able to continue playing on the weekend, he was also guaranteed his first paycheck from a big-time American tournament.

To John Daly's mind, though, the most important event that occurred that weekend transpired on the driving range. Daly's swing was still as long as it had been back at Helias High School, but by now that additional shoulder turn and clubhead speed were beginning to produce tangible results. He could fly the ball pretty long and especially high, and some of the other golfers occasionally noticed this. On this day Daly looked up from smashing a sizable drive and froze in place. Jack Nicklaus was standing on the driving range, not twenty feet away, and he was watching.

Thank God that Nicklaus didn't say hi again, or anything else that would have required Daly to respond. He was having enough trouble resisting the urge to run; anything more and he would have been struck mute again. Being the world's most accomplished golfer, Nicklaus had the aplomb to know just what to do. He winked. Daly was jubilant.

Nicklaus went about his business, hitting balls and working on his game. Daly watched him surreptitiously, not even considering going over and introducing himself. Nicklaus played far too complicated a role in Daly's psyche for him to risk something like that. The list of stupid things he could imagine himself saying or doing would fill reams of paper.

When Nicklaus finished his practice session, he watched Daly hit a few more balls. As Nicklaus was about to leave, he caught Daly's eye and winked again.

Daly would go on to shoot 80, then 79, over the weekend, completing the tournament at twenty over. Such amateurish scores hardly fazed him. He had earned $4,099 in the big leagues, and Jack Nicklaus had winked at him—twice.

$$\left(\,5\,\right)$$

Over the Edge

 John Daly received a sponsor exemption to play in the St. Jude Classic in August 1989. It was a bona fide PGA Tour event, held in an upscale suburb east of Memphis called Germantown. Since he hadn't won playing privileges yet, one of Daly's few hopes for gaining entry to sanctioned events was by obtaining one of the handful of slots the tour gives to local tournament organizers. Daly had finagled only four such invitations so far in 1989, but he didn't let that restrain his goals at the St. Jude. He went to Memphis with one intention: He was aiming to be in contention to win the tournament come Sunday afternoon.

Although he could now drive the ball three hundred yards with some regularity—which was longer than most professionals—Daly's game was wildly erratic. He had a tendency to spray balls all over the course and to follow terrific rounds with disastrous ones. He seldom got to play at well-attended tournaments, and he had never been in contention at one in the United States. More than anything, this meant that he hadn't had a chance to hold and blow a lead in a tournament and then get over it the following week. This was a nearly mandatory step on the path to becoming a tournament winner.

By not being in contention at a tournament since returning from South Africa earlier in the year, Daly had also been denied the mass applause he had acquired a taste for on the Sunshine Tour. That was assuaged minimally when he played at Memphis, which is situated opposite Arkansas on the Mississippi River. Daly managed to draw an appreciative gallery of several dozen friends and family members there. His wife, Dale, was among them, even though it required heroic measures to get her there. Several days before, she had had surgery to repair torn ligaments in her knee, and she had to navigate the course in a golf cart, something that was possible only because there were so few people following her husband's group.

If Dale was happy to see her husband getting the chance to play in a PGA Tour event, she couldn't have been overly pleased about the new friends he made there. John had played a practice round at the tournament with Fuzzy Zoeller and Hubert Green, two journeyman tour members who each had over $2 million in career earnings. Green was forty-two and had won nineteen tournaments, including two majors. Zoeller, thirty-seven, had won ten tournaments, also including two majors.

Zoeller was one of the funniest and most outgoing men in golf. He could fire off one-liners at a furious pace, and he felt he had an obligation to entertain the golf fans who came out to see him. He was extremely low-key on the course, often trading quips with his gallery as he played tournament rounds, while all around him his fellow competitors were staring sternly ahead. Fuzzy liked to win as much as anyone, but he never forgot that it was, after all, just golf.

Zoeller and Daly felt an instant kinship with each other. Part of that was temperament. Both men were irreverent and rebellious by nature, and they were skilled in the fine art of agitating those who lived by the rules they disdained. Neither had any pretensions about themselves or what they did for a living. They were highly social and loved a good time. More ominously, they also shared a reputation as being frequent and heavy drinkers.

Daly made the two-day cut at the St. Jude, then went flat on the weekend, shooting a 78 and a 73 to finish tied for sixty-fourth place. The ride back to Blytheville was less than a hundred miles, but it must have seemed longer. John had missed another rare opportunity to perform well in a PGA Tour event, and Dale's knee made it difficult for her to get comfortable in a car.

Before the Dalys could get any rest that night, a call came in at 11:30 P.M. There was an opening for Monday morning in the Insurance Youth Golf Classic, a small tournament that was being held in Texarkana, 325 miles away in the far southwestern corner of Arkansas. Money was money; Daly said he'd be there. He left Blytheville at 3 A.M. and arrived five and a half hours later.

After having spent more time driving than sleeping that night, Daly got a slow start and found another member of his foursome beating him by four shots after nine holes. To Daly's chagrin, he was being outshot by a thirteen-year-old kid named Tiger Woods. Like Daly when he was a teenager, Woods was a gifted boy golfer who was acquiring a reputation for beating adults. Daly didn't like this kid's turning the tables on him, and he especially didn't like that everyone was applauding Woods while no one was clapping for him. He got serious and beat Woods by two shots.

Getting appreciation from the gallery was not a problem later that month when Daly got a sponsor exemption into the Chattanooga Classic in southeastern Tennessee. He shot three phenomenal rounds of 65, 66, and 63 at the Chattanooga Classic before ballooning to a final-round 74. After leading the tournament at times, he finished fourteenth. Rather than seeing three good days of golf, Daly focused on one bad day and went into a funk.

When Daly got depressed at times like these, he would medicate himself with massive quantities of alcohol, as he'd done that year when he and his brother, Jamie, had gone drinking in Centerville, Arkansas, a blink-and-you-missed-it burg of four hundred that lay due south of Dardanelle. There was a little bar complete with pool tables, over by the race course for dirt-track cars. It was a Dardanelle hangout.

John's standby drink was triple Jack with a splash of Coke: three shots of Jack Daniel's sweetened with a little spill of Coke in the glass. On a righteous night, John could finish off an entire bottle of Jack Daniel's using this prescription.

On this particular evening, however, John was drinking beer and a bit of Jack as a complement to much larger quantities of Bacardi rum. John liked to say that when he was drinking seriously, he would consume enough alcohol before dinner to keep most people drunk for two days. That night in Centerville, he quaffed enough to tank the entire town for a week.

The rage that alcohol released in John Daly was so intense that sometimes he tried to destroy his surroundings, as though objects were representations of the demons that haunted him. In college it had been dorm rooms; around Dardanelle it often involved cars. Daly had lashed out at the windshields and mirrors of several motor vehicles with his fists, and he had once ripped a seat clear out of a friend's van.

Other times, he would get into a car—with passengers— and see how many consecutive red lights he could run at full speed in traffic, wooing death. He used a modification of that approach coming back from Centerville, his belly sloshing with rum. John was piloting a Chevy Blazer from the 1980s—a bloated Jeep-like vehicle with the aerodynamics of a clothes washer and enough ground clearance to pass over a tree stump. When this machine was caked with a veneer of dried red clay overlaying a mass of strategic dents, it seemed so at home in the backwoods of Arkansas that it appeared to be a product of the natural rather than the manufactured world.

With Jamie riding shotgun, John was pushing the Blazer fast up Highway 7 toward Dardanelle. The two-lane road sliced through farmers' fields like a balance beam, with the raised surface of the road falling off precipitously at the shoulders. There were three-foot drainage ditches bordering the blacktop, and they caught everything that dropped off it.

When John let the wheels on the right side of the Blazer drift over the edge of the road, the tires caught in the drainage ditch, launching the vehicle into the air, where it began to tumble as if in a scene from an action-adventure movie. The vehicle rolled into a farmer's bean field, ejecting Jamie out an open window during one of the revolutions. John was tossed across the seat and stayed along for the ride.

When he pulled stunts like this, there were plenty of times when John didn't think he would survive. But, as was the case this early morning, he always did. He crawled out of the battered vehicle, past the bent-up golf clubs that had flown around inside, and discovered that neither he nor Jamie was hurt. The only real impact of the incident was the freshly crumpled look the Blazer took on—giving it a sort of rustic *je ne sais quoi.*

The boys brushed themselves off and looked around. There wasn't a soul in sight, and it was so quiet you could hear the night crawlers crawl. Dardanelle was over six miles north, but they knew what they had to do—get away from the vehicle in case the police arrived. The Daly boys set off for home, putting one foot wearily in front of the other as they trudged along Highway 7, their path illuminated by the stars.

John's mother, Lou, was the glue that kept her family together through every crisis like this. After John had been in an accident or been hospitalized or gone into a depression after playing badly in a tournament, he'd sneak down the hill in Dardanelle to the cow pasture he had turned into Wildcat Hollow Driving Range. He'd stand there, the way he used to do before his life got complicated, and whack balls. Lou would come down into the peaceful valley, where the rest of the world seemed eons away, and have long talks with her son about how he had to stop drinking like this. Did he want to kill himself?

John would straighten up for a short time—until the next predicament arose. Then he would escape it by embarking upon another horrendous drunk. He went on the most extended drunk of his young life that fall, when Dale decided that she had had enough. This wasn't what she had bargained for. It was time to get a divorce. The marriage was never meant to be, and there were no children to slow the healing of the wound. The blame of one could be arranged to cancel out the blame of the other, and everybody could walk away clean.

John couldn't do it that way. He had to see it as another in the endless series of fuck-ups he called his life.

Although it required a Herculean effort, Daly began drinking even more. In December he paid a visit to a friend of his, Don Cline. Cline, who was nearing sixty, had moved to Dardanelle from New Jersey eight years before for the quiet. Daly recruited Cline as another in the series of smart and generous mentors/big brothers/father figures that he managed to lure into his life. With his tremendous talent and even larger vulnerability, Daly always found people who wanted to help him. Cline became a member at the Bay Ridge Boat and Golf Club, and he and John would hit balls and have talks. Sometimes Daly would seek him out when he needed advice.

When Daly came to see Cline in December, it was a professional call. Cline was the administrator of Dardanelle Hospital, and Daly was there to be admitted to his institution with a blood alcohol level of .27, nearly three times the legal definition of intoxication in most states. Daly, depressed over his failed marriage, his inability to become the leading player on the PGA Tour overnight, and even his drinking, was checking himself in for two days of drying out. He told friends that he realized his life was out of control but that he doubted he could do anything about it.

At the beginning of January, Daly finished first in a qualifying tournament for a new minor-league tour that was starting in the United States in early spring. With his divorce moving through the courts, Daly was rooming with Blake Allison, a drinking buddy from Morrilton, Arkansas. Daly decided to spend the winter playing the Sunshine Tour again, and this time he took Allison with him.

Daly played decently through January, finishing in the top thirty at the three tournaments he entered. Then in February he arrived in Johannesburg and the Rand Park Golf Club. They like their tournament golf courses long in South Africa, and Rand Park was a monster at 7,320 yards. Other than its distance, though, it was a benign course with minimal hazards to waylay imprudent golfers. It was a layout after the heart of the man whose definition of how to play golf was: Hit the ball as hard as you can, walk quickly to where the ball stops, and hit it again as hard as you can.

Daly's tremendous length was beginning to be noticed in South Africa now that it was his second year there and he was becoming a regular contender. He was no longer just another visiting American. He was that American boy who seemed to hit the ball farther than anyone they had ever seen. His galleries were growing at every tournament, particularly at a course such as Rand Park, where Daly could whale away with his driver with abandon.

Playing as aggressively as he ever had, Daly was seven shots off the lead after two days at Rand Park. Then he came roaring out with a 62, matching the course record. He was tied for the lead when he came to the final hole of the tournament, needing to make a 12-foot birdie putt to win. When he slipped the ball into the side of the cup, Daly showed he had both the short game and the nerves to win.

The tournament victory was a tremendous boost for Daly's self-confidence, while the $16,000 first prize was pure profit. Daly was financing his own trip this year, so he didn't have to share the proceeds with anyone. Added to the $3,700 he had won during January, Daly was building up a significant financial cushion to take back to the States. Although he would probably be able to get another half-dozen sponsor exemptions on the PGA Tour, he would be spending most of the coming year playing low-stakes events, while encountering significant travel costs. Having money to fall back on would relieve a lot of the pressure.

Two weeks after his first South African victory, Daly and Allison rolled into Swaziland, home of the Swazi Sun Classic. Although a different course was being used that year, Daly had finished second in this tournament the previous season, and that was always a good omen. True to form, Daly completed his first round in 66 strokes—just before a violent hailstorm descended on the course.

Gambling was legal in Swaziland, and John Daly was discovering that, taken to the proper degree of excess, a night at the casino could offer every bit as much excitement as a drunken tear in a Chevy Blazer. Given the way his luck was going on the golf course, how could some of it not rub off at the gaming tables? Making a trip to the casino under such circumstances was, for John Daly, the personal equivalent of Manifest Destiny. It was practically preordained.

Daly's fortunes that evening ran in inverse proportion to

the amount he drank. As the amount of alcohol he consumed and the time he spent at the tables increased, the amount of money in his pocket decreased. By dawn he had consumed massive quantities of alcohol while managing to piss away much of the money he had won on the Sunshine Tour. A month's work, built upon years of preparation, and with the potential to underwrite the coming season in the States, was gone—just like that.

As the horrible truth of it all penetrated his alcoholic daze, Daly managed to contain his rage until he got back to his hotel room, where he erupted, damaging himself and his surroundings. When he calmed down, Daly called Rick Ross, his friend back in Dardanelle. Daly would call Ross at least once a month, regardless of where he was. When he was playing really well, he would call every week. If there was trouble, he would call less frequently. Often the emergency calls came when Daly had gotten himself into a situation he couldn't handle, but he wouldn't ask for help until the last possible minute.

It was the early hours of the morning in Arkansas, but getting close to tee time in Swaziland, when Ross was awakened by the phone. He picked it up and heard John Daly's voice coming over the line.

"I need to talk to you," Daly said. "I kind of hit the door and my hand is busted up. Shit, I don't know if I can play. What do I do? Do I withdraw? Do I try to make it through?"

Ross's advice was to get medical attention and ask the doctor if it was possible for him to continue. That was how Daly came to show up on the first tee with his hand stitched and bandaged. The South African golfer Wayne Player told Tom Callahan of the *Washington Post* that the other golfers were astounded that Daly was going to try playing like that.

Daly told Player he had no choice. "I lost so much money at the casino," he said, "that I have to win the tournament now just to break even."

To the amazement of everyone but John Daly, he shot a 71 straight out of the emergency room. The next day he shot a 64, putting him three strokes off the lead. He birdied five of the first nine holes in the final round, reaching the seventeenth hole tied with the leader, John Bland, one of the premier players in South Africa. Bland lost his tee shot out of bounds and took a double bogey, handing Daly a two-shot lead in the tournament. All Daly—with stitches still in his hand, and his bank account vaporized—had to do was take an easy par and move on to recover $16,000 of his losses.

To do so, however, would mean passing up the exquisite pleasure of being microns away from losing everything—of having your heart pound and your breath come in gulps and your mouth go parchment dry. All of these irresistible tests were, in their own way, little sprints through the jaws of death. Escaping from them unscathed let Daly feel—for the briefest of moments—like the King of the Freaking World.

That's how John Daly felt when, needing par, and risking it all, he shot for the flag. Going flat out was all that he knew. It worked. He dropped his first putt for birdie and, rather than having somebody give him a two-shot lead, he created his own three-shot lead. That was his victory margin one hole later. Daly rolled out of town with his second win in three weeks. His hand was mending, and even with the damages at the hotel, he was only slightly poorer than when he had arrived.

Then he finished third in two tournaments in March and won another $13,000. Any second thoughts John Daly might have had about his lifestyle were quickly erased when his dazzling performance on the Sunshine Tour got him invited to the South African Skins Game. Skins Games are made-for-TV golf matches that are played throughout the world. Their format of awarding large sums of cash to the winner of each hole in an eighteen-hole match rather than to the person with the overall low score rewards risk-takers, as Daly proved. Playing in his first Skins Game, he picked up $35,000.

Daly was propelled back to the United States by a wave of exhilaration. What more could a man ask for? Here was this twenty-four-year-old dude from Dardanelle, hopping on an airplane with his golf clubs, going to Africa of all places, playing a little golf, having a serious good time, and, as the pièce de résistance, winning, losing, then winning back all this goddamn money. As John Daly winged back over the Atlantic, Frank Sinatra seemed to be somewhere over the horizon, drink in one hand, cigarette in the other, singing, "I did it my way."

Breaking News

When John Daly arrived back in the United States, he was determined that things were going to be different this year. He was brimming with self-confidence, and he had a new venue to conquer. He was going to be playing on the Ben Hogan Tour, which was a minor-league version of the PGA Tour. Some cities without PGA Tour events wanted to host a golf tournament, and many young American golfers didn't want to have to play overseas to acquire experience in high-level competition. These two needs were answered simultaneously when the PGA Tour office convinced Cosmo World of Japan, the owner of the Ben Hogan golf equipment company, to put up $20 million over five years to be the title sponsor of the new series.

The Hogan Tour was going to consist of thirty three-day tournaments with $100,000 purses, $20,000 of which would go to the winner of the event. By American professional golf standards, this was small change, especially when 132 golfers were going to be competing for it. After all the computations were done, there were going to be a number of golfers each week who made the cut but whose earnings reached only the high three figures.

The real draw of the Hogan Tour was the entry it offered fifty golfers to the PGA Tour. The top five money-winners for the year were going to receive one-year exemptions on the PGA Tour, and those in the sixth through fiftieth spots would be able to skip various portions of the annual PGA Tour Qualifying Tournament.

If he had any question about which player was going to own the Hogan Tour, Daly only had to look at his record. Since January, he had won the Hogan Qualifying Tournament. He had won twice on the Sunshine Tour, and he had cleaned up at the South African Skins Game. If he needed a mantra when he was on a roll like this, he only had to fall back on the one he used on the golf team at Helias High: *I am unstoppable. No one can touch me.*

Daly had a lot of time to recall the old days as he traveled around on the Hogan Tour. He, like most of the other golfers, was driving from tournament to tournament. It was all anybody could afford, and Daly didn't like to fly, anyway. Having a car also served another need. If things were not going too well and he got too drunk at night, he could sleep in his car in the golf course parking lot so he wouldn't miss his tee time the next morning. It wouldn't be the first time Daly played a round of golf in an alcohol mist—either still drunk or hung over from the night before. This never seemed to affect his performance on the course.

The Hogan Tour rolled into Macon, Georgia, at the end of April 1990, and while Daly was at the course one day his eye was caught by a short, trim woman with blondish hair that was long enough to require fussing with. She was pretty, with strong cheekbones and a tight mouth. She said her name was Bettye Fulford and that she worked in convention sales for the local Radisson Hotel. As a former cheerleader from Georgia Southern College at Statesboro, she had good enthusiasm. John Daly was a newly single man, and he was falling in love again.

Bettye claimed she was thirty, but that didn't seem to jive with the lines that appeared at the corners of her eyes when she smiled or the uneven quality of the skin on the back of her hands. John, who had just turned twenty-four, didn't question it. That wouldn't have been very polite, especially since when John and Bettye went out and he drank, she didn't ask if he had an alcohol problem. If anyone else raised the issue, she'd say he was working on his image as a party animal, then smile benevolently. John talked to Bettye about what had happened with Dale, and Bettye allowed that yes, she'd been married once as well.

John and Bettye started hanging out then, and as the weeks passed and John's buddies got to meet Bettye, they'd get John alone and whisper that there was no way this woman was thirty. John would say that he was having a very, very good time with Bettye, if you caught his drift, and that he didn't understand why they were having this conversation. He was free, and Bettye was both pretty and eager to please. What was the problem here? It wasn't like he was going to marry her.

Daly was especially in need of the companionship Bettye provided that summer because, as the Hogan Tour reached the middle of its season in July, he was only thirtieth on the money list, with $15,858 in earnings. He hadn't won a tournament, and he certainly wasn't getting rich. Sure, he could hustle to make extra money, such as the $500 he might win at a long-drive contest at a tournament. And he could sometimes get free lodging and meals in local homes at tournament sites. But this kind of life wasn't what Daly had devoted so many years to golf for.

He had won all these amateur tournaments as a kid, he had won twice in South Africa a few months before, and now it was time for him to be winning regularly in the States—but it wasn't happening!

It wasn't supposed to be playing out like this. According to the plan, he was supposed to be a headliner by now. Since he wasn't, he could only conclude that it was his fault. Daly began losing all desire to play golf, and he even thought about quitting the game. If he couldn't win, he'd rather not compete at all.

Daly's depression reached its nadir in the middle of July when he shot a round of 91 at the New England Classic in Falmouth, Maine. It was a score Daly had last recorded when he was about ten years old, and he snapped. He told Hogan Tour officials and several reporters that he was broke—although he had won significant money in South Africa only months before—and that he didn't know how much longer he could hold on.

That night he went drinking in a local bar with his friend and fellow competitor Roger Rowland and a number of other players from the tournament. It was already common knowledge on the Hogan Tour that Daly had a drinking problem, but he outdid himself that night. Revisiting his old standby of Jack and Coke, Daly went on a tear that ended only when he passed out. Roger Rowland, who hadn't been through this drill before, was terrified. He rushed Daly to the hospital, where they got out the stomach pump.

When he regained consciousness, Daly called Don Cline at the hospital in Dardanelle. Cline told him that he was too gifted to wallow in self-pity and that he had to take responsibility for himself. His drinking was just another form of making excuses, Cline said, and nothing was going to change until he stopped. That wasn't what Daly had called to hear.

He called Rick Ross, who listened sympathetically but didn't react too strongly one way or the other. Ross had been down this road with Daly too many times over the last seven years. He knew nothing was going to change until Daly hit bottom, and at this point all he wanted Daly to do was to hurry up and get there so he could start getting better. Ross used to pray that Daly would play golf so badly when he was hung over that he would never make another cut. He believed that was the only thing that would motivate him to stop.

Then Daly called Bettye Fulford and said he'd almost

drunk himself to death. She shrieked and said she'd be on the next plane north. When Bettye arrived, John said he was thinking about quitting golf. Bettye said he was too good to quit. John said if that was true, she should relinquish her job at the Radisson and come on the road with him. She bought it.

John and Bettye went to Hilton Head, South Carolina, so that John could chill out. When he was sufficiently relaxed, Bettye sat him down and gave him a good talking-to. She said she had decided to set some priorities for his life, and she ticked off some of the things he was going to have to change to meet them. As far as Bettye was concerned, she was trying to put John's life in perspective for him. She felt that having clearly defined priorities was essential.

Daly went along with this, and on his own he committed to making what he thought was an enormous change. He decided that, because every time he had been hospitalized he had been drinking hard liquor as his main course, he was going to give it up cold. No more Jack Daniel's for John Daly. From now on, he was strictly a beer man.

Something right happened in South Carolina, because when Daly came back to golf in early August, he played the best he had since South Africa. He obtained another sponsor exemption to the St. Jude Classic and finished tied for twenty-first, shooting four solid rounds and winning $9,388. It was his biggest check ever on the PGA Tour.

Returning to the Hogan Tour in early September, he finished second at the Texarkana Open. The following week he tied for second at the Amarillo Open. The week after that, it finally happened. He won his first Hogan event—the Utah Open. By the end of the season in October, he was ninth on the Hogan money list. He had taken in $65,646 and earned a bye directly into the final round of the PGA Tour Qualifying Tournament in December.

Daly traveled to Palm Springs, California, for that tournament and skated to a tie for twelfth place. That accomplishment was enough to virtually guarantee that he would be able to play in every PGA Tour event he wanted to during 1991. Three years after he had left the University of Arkansas, and after grossing over $150,000 in 1990, John Daly was headed for the big time.

The first thing Daly did after his successful run of tournaments was to buy a $120,000 house for him and Bettye in Cordova, a suburb east of Memphis. He also hired a carpenter to build a trophy case for the house in preparation for the glories to come. Daly was only twenty-four, and he had bought a house for his woman and himself with his own money.

When that situation was under control, Daly got on the phone and called Fuzzy Zoeller. Daly told him about winning his playing privileges and asked Zoeller for a special favor. He wanted to know if Fuzzy would be his big brother—show him around at different tournament stops and be there for him when he needed some advice.

Zoeller, like other men before him, was disarmed by the forthrightness and ingenuousness of Daly's request. No one had ever helped Zoeller when he came along, and he liked the idea of fixing that with somebody else. The other thing was, with Zoeller's reputation as a man who knew how to have a good time, on a tour that wasn't known as a party circuit, he wasn't the first guy young players thought of when they were looking for a mentor.

Plenty of guys liked Fuzzy, but instead of a big brother, they tended to think of him as a delinquent uncle. So he had some time on his hands, as it were, when it came to serving as a role model. Plus he genuinely liked John, who was certainly going to be a one-of-a-kind article on the tour. "Hell, yes," Zoeller told Daly, "come on around. I'll corrupt your little brain for you."

With his first full year on the PGA Tour not scheduled to begin until the second week of January, John Daly decided that he didn't feel like hanging around with nothing to do for most of December 1990. Even though the airfare was hefty, Daly told Bettye to pack a suitcase. They were going to blow over to South Africa and hit a few stops on the Sunshine Tour.

Daly loved to play golf in South Africa. The galleries were bigger than they were on the Hogan Tour, there was television coverage, and in December it was warmer than Tennessee. Besides, John had taken a beating in the casinos there the year before, and he had some monetary scores to settle.

Once they got to South Africa, Daly decided he was ready for some serious action at the casinos late one night, but Bettye was tired, so she told John to go on by himself while she went to bed. When she awoke in the morning, John was standing there, bleary-eyed, with $40,000 in cash in his hands.

Daly had spent the whole night playing blackjack, but rather than having hit it big, he had actually come out ahead by only a modest sum. Before he got hot, Daly had been down almost the entire $40,000. While other golfers were spending the night resting up for the final round, Daly was scrambling to save himself from financial disaster.

He dumped the cash on the bed and told Bettye to find a bank that would convert the bills into a certified check for the trip home. While John went off to play in a golf tournament with some of the best professionals in the world, Bettye walked the streets with huge bundles of bills stuffed into her clothes like a bank robber on the lam.

The statisticians of the PGA Tour were waiting for Daly when he returned to the States. The PGA Tour keeps a multitude of statistics on its players and tournaments, and after participating in only three events, Daly was at the top of one of their categories: driving distance. He was averaging 295 yards with his driver, while the next-best pro was well back at 283.

In February he even managed to pick up an agent. Daly had met Bud Martin in Memphis the year before. He was a young guy who was starting a new agency with another man, and a mutual friend introduced Daly and Martin at the Chickasaw Country Club, where Daly was beginning to hang out.

Daly didn't have playing privileges on the PGA Tour then, so Martin couldn't do much for him. Then they met again at a tournament in San Diego in early 1991, and Daly signed on with Martin's agency for two years.

As Martin looked around for endorsement deals or corporate outings for Daly, Bettye Fulford was continuing her efforts to get him sober and motivated. Bettye subscribed to the theory that drinking was encouraged by inactivity, so she concocted a rehabilitation program that had exertion as its keystone. After John came home from a day at the golf course—and a stop at McDonald's for two double cheeseburgers, large fries, and a diet Coke—Bettye hauled him off to play tennis all night. She hoped that by depriving him of the time and energy he needed to drink, he'd lose his taste for it as well.

Daly went along with Bettye's program enthusiastically at first. He was given to telling friends unbidden about the terrific evening he had spent on the tennis court or about how he really was acquiring a taste for that Dr Pepper. Daly's drinking buddies would look askance at these pronouncements, hearing Bettye's voice in them instructing John that he had to take steps to change his image now that he was on the PGA Tour.

The drinking buddies flat-out didn't like Bettye, but she didn't fret about that. She planned to thin their ranks considerably, anyway. The drinking buddies felt themselves being sized up when they were around Bettye. She was figuring who could stay and who couldn't. If Bettye thought one of them was someone who would talk to John privately and try to turn him against her, then she would take action to sever that relationship. When any of the drinking buddies saw her doing that kind of manipulating, they'd start treating her like dirt—right in front of John, so he'd know how they felt.

Not that there weren't people on Bettye's side. There were those in John's family who thought she was just what he needed to settle him down. The hope was that Bettye would remove the distractions that were keeping John from the big time. Don Cline, at Dardanelle Hospital, recognized that Bettye was older than John but believed that her maturity would do wonders for him. Even Steve Loy, his old coach from the University of Arkansas, thought Bettye was a wonderful influence on John—and he had seen the boy at his wildest.

One thing Bettye was worried about was the new environment they were traveling in on the PGA Tour. She could handle the good ol' boys from Arkansas and those from their new home, Tennessee. She had spent her life around such men, and since she was the one who went home with John at night, she usually didn't feel overly threatened by them.

But guys like Fuzzy Zoeller . . . now that was another matter. They were the royalty of golf—rich, famous, and always in demand. There were far more guys on the tour who went to Bible study than went bar-hopping. Nonetheless, a charming guy like Zoeller slipping into a new country club every week could, just by showing up, create a scene that was intoxicating in manifold ways. To a twenty-five-year-old party boy who had spent most of his time dreaming about being a PGA star, it could seem as though he had stumbled into a rock video come to life.

Bettye brooded over this but didn't say anything about it until they were in Florida at the Honda Classic in March. John had started the season slowly, missing the cut in half the six tournaments he entered and earning about $15,000. In addition to needing money to live on and make mortgage payments with, Daly also had to win money—or a tournament—to keep his playing privileges for 1992. Those who finished in the top 125 on the money list were excused from the qualifying tournament;

everybody else who didn't have an exemption as a result of winning a tournament had to go back.

As golfers are wont to do, Daly suddenly got hot at the Honda, shooting two rounds of 68 to put him among the leaders of the event in Coral Springs, Florida, going into the weekend. Daly's performance won him a larger than normal gallery on the course, although since he was still an unknown in the States, the number of people who would follow him was minimal compared with the throngs who trailed after Australian superstar Greg Norman.

Norman was the self-styled, platinum blond Great White Shark of golf. A tall, handsome man with a talent for self-promotion, he hit the ball farther and played more aggressively than many other men on the tour, and golf fans responded to that. Norman didn't win tournaments that frequently on the American tour, but he was in contention often and therefore was exciting to watch.

That weekend Norman, who was playing in the group ahead of Daly at the Honda Classic, found himself standing on the seventeenth fairway, waiting for the putting green to clear so he could hit his second shot. A tournament marshal standing near Norman turned back and saw Daly waiting on the tee for a signal to hit. The marshal didn't know who Daly was, but he felt certain that whoever he was, he assuredly couldn't hit the ball as far as the Great White Shark. The marshal signaled Daly to hit.

Daly's ball almost struck Norman on the fly, traveling ten yards beyond him before it touched the ground and began to roll, stopping 320 yards from the tee. People in Norman's gallery stared at each other in disbelief. Who was that back there who just blew a golf ball well past the Shark? They didn't know, but a few of them peeled off to give Daly a once-over on the next tee. When he demolished another drive, they hooted and hollered in appreciation, something that didn't happen often to obscure golfers. Daly smiled awkwardly back at them.

When Bettye Fulford, who had been walking in John's gallery, observed this, she turned to a reporter who was accompanying her. "David," she said, "this happens whenever he's hitting the ball well. The fans go nuts."

David was David Lanier, a sportswriter from the *Arkansas Gazette*. Lanier, a Louisiana native, had already written several stories about Daly, and he knew Bettye well enough to consider her a friend. She seemed like a nice woman to him, even if she had, rather oddly, asked Lanier to identify her in the newpaper as Bettye Blackshear, saying that was a name from a former marriage.

It was a terrific break for Lanier that Daly was doing so well in the tournament, as Lanier was in the midst of writing a major story about John. Newspapers in Arkansas had been covering Daly's golf career routinely since he was in college, and that was especially true of the *Gazette*. Lanier's paper and its competitor, the *Arkansas Democrat*, were in a fight to the death. Both were losing money, and would continue to lose money, until one or the other went out of business. There wasn't room in Arkansas for two statewide newspapers any longer.

As one of its tactics in the circulation battle, the *Gazette* was emphasizing its sports coverage, and since some of the paper's sports editors were avid golf fans, golf coverage especially was being increased. Lanier's paper wouldn't ordinarily have sent him to Florida to attend a tournament, but since he was in the state covering baseball spring training, he'd gotten approval to hop over to the Honda Classic.

Bettye knew that Lanier was working on a long story about John, and as they walked the course she brought Lanier up to date on the tournaments John had played and how he had finished. Lanier asked how Daly was holding up under the considerable pressures of playing on the PGA Tour.

"David," Bettye said, "I'm concerned about the bad influence guys on the tour are having on John. He drinks way too much when he hangs around with fellows like Fuzzy Zoeller."

Lanier was stunned. This was the first he had heard about John Daly having a drinking problem. Astonishingly, with the major role alcohol had played in Daly's life, his friends, family, and teammates had managed to keep Daly's illness to themselves. Now that Bettye had served this information up to Lanier while he was researching a story, he was going to follow up on it, of course.

Lanier caught up with Daly in the tournament's pressroom after his round. The golfer seemed shocked when Lanier told him what Bettye had said about his drinking too much. Lanier asked if it was true. Daly said that he liked to drink sometimes, but volunteered only one story about any excesses. He said that he had been admitted to Dardanelle Hospital in December of 1989 after being on a binge.

"I took it too far," he said. "I had had some problem with my drinking, but I thought it could help me deal with some things I was going through. There are still times I'll have a beer. I quit drinking hard liquor.

"The priorities," he said proudly. "I think I have them in order."

Lest he leave Lanier with the impression that alcohol was a problem for him, Daly added: "Some of my best rounds came when I was hung over. It's not something I brag on. It's not something I want to encourage young kids to do. It was something I struggled with."

The pressroom at a golf tournament is a busy place near the end of the day's competition, as the golfers leading the tournament come in for interviews and newspaper reporters hurry to write stories on deadline. Most of the interviews that take place there are done press-conference style, without any privacy. Even when a writer is talking to a golfer one-on-one, other reporters think nothing of coming over and joining in. It's part of the culture, and usually not a problem, as newspaper reporters seldom have overlapping readerships. But as David Lanier sat there asking John Daly about his drinking habits, they were ignored. Few people outside of Arkansas knew—or cared—who John Daly was, so there wasn't a story there for anyone else.

While Daly was talking to Lanier, he decided that it might be a good time to surreptitiously express to his agent that he was displeased with his performance without Daly having to say so to the agent's face. He could have Lanier do it for him in the newspaper. Not telling Lanier that he had an agent, Daly began complaining about his lack of off-course income. "I might be the only guy on the tour with no endorsements on my golf bag," he said. "That could bring in fifty thousand dollars a year. What am I getting? Nothing, absolutely zilch. I don't know why no one has called. I've wondered about it. I guess all I can do is wait. I'm sure I'm going to get a good deal one of these days."

Lanier went on to talk to Fuzzy Zoeller, although to Bettye's disappointment he didn't ask Zoeller if he was a bad influence on Daly. Lanier figured that, at twenty-five, Daly was old enough to take care of himself. Zoeller said that he liked John and enjoyed his company, but otherwise Zoeller's assessment was the same as everyone else's: John Daly had to get real with his expectations—he was a kid on his first year on the PGA Tour, for God's sake. What had happened when he was sixteen didn't mean squat. Everybody on the tour had been a boy-wonder golfer.

"The key for John," Fuzzy said, "is to keep making the cuts and beating on the door, and eventually the door is going to open. Do that, and sooner or later he'll win. But for now he needs to just not rush it—don't push the red button too early."

Daly came close to proving Zoeller—and everybody else—wrong at the Honda Classic. He finished tied for fourth and won a very substantial $41,333. Two weeks later he picked up another $14,500 in New Orleans. It was only March, and he had won over $70,000 in eight tournaments.

A guy still had to hustle, though, so when Daly went back to Arkansas in April to play in a charity tournament at Chenal Country Club in Little Rock, he asked the folks there if they might not be interested in sponsoring him. It was common for golfers to represent a specific country club or a gated golf community. They'd attend events there and display the club's name on their golf bag in exchange for cash. The people at Chenal told Daly that it was a right interesting proposition he had there and that they'd get back to him as soon as they could.

In the meantime, John and Bettye went on a blitz, traveling every week and playing in seven consecutive tournaments without a rest. When they finally relented, in June, it was to take a trip that John had been anticipating for months. They went to Las Vegas. Part of the allure was gambling. John Daly loved to gamble as much as he had loved biscuits with chocolate sauce when he was fifteen in Jefferson City. Yet there was a more compelling aspect of the trip for Daly. After having spent a year with her, he had decided it was time to make Bettye his wife.

The last time Daly had gotten married, he had done it with as much fanfare as could be mustered in Blytheville. He had never seen so much fussing over anything in his life, and what did it change? As far as he was concerned, getting married was like hitting a golf ball. You gave it a look, a waggle, then *bam*—you did it. John Daly would tell you that the surest way of screwing up a golf swing—or anything, really—was to spend too much time thinking about it. Even worse was talking about it. Daly believed God wouldn't have given us impulses if He hadn't wanted us to respond to them.

And what a place Vegas was to get married in. There might have been as many wedding chapels as casinos. You never had to drive far to find one. Or they would come and pick you up if you wanted. They could supply Elvis impersonators as witnesses or lead you through your vows at a drive-up window. They really knew how to marry people in Las Vegas wedding chapels, because it was their only job. They were specialists—no funerals, baptisms, or Easter services. Best of all, you could dress as you wished, and you didn't have to invite people and be amicable to them afterward.

The wedding was John's deal, so he picked the place and everything. But one part of it was kind of strange. Bettye was holding back some. He knew she loved him—she said it all the time, just as he did. There was just something going on with her about this. John had made up his mind, though, and they did show up at the chapel. Bettye kept acting nervous and mysterious, getting John annoyed. Then, before the ceremony started, she said she couldn't do it, and ran out. John let her off, but only for a few months. They were coming back to Vegas in October to play in a tournament, and they would get married then. Bettye said fine, fine, but not now. She wasn't ready.

They went back to Memphis, and John played in the St. Jude again. With him and Bettye living right there outside Memphis, Lou and Jim Daly came down from Dardanelle, and a squad of other family and friends showed up with overnight bags. Bettye smiled and told people that sure, she had a houseful, but John loved it and it helped him relax. Rick Ross came over and helped John work on his swing. There were people from the Chenal Country Club who had come to Memphis for the tournament, and Daly asked whether they had decided to sponsor him. They said they were still thinking on it but they'd let him know.

It was a hectic week, but John needed whatever diversions he could find, because he was once again a golfing fool. After returning from Vegas, he was scheduled for another succession of seven events. Even though he was playing so frequently, Daly had a tremendous July, picking up $70,000 more in three weeks.

By mid-August Daly was posting tremendous numbers for a rookie. Of the thirty tournaments held, he had played in twenty-four of them and made the cut in thirteen. He was seventy-second on the money list, with $166,650 in earnings, and would almost certainly finish in the top 125 by the end of the year. He was still first in driving distance, with a 286-yard average. All in all, it wouldn't have been hard for him to justify taking some time off, especially since he didn't have much chance of getting into the next tournament, the PGA Championship.

The PGA Championship was the final of the year's four majors, and it was run by the association of teaching pros from golf clubs around the country: the PGA of America, not the PGA Tour. The PGA of America allowed forty or more of its members to play in the event with the touring pros from the PGA Tour—a quarter of the field. Some professional golfers felt this weakened the tournament, and it caused them to waver about whether they were going to play, putting off the decision until the last minute.

Daly's only shot at getting into the tournament was to sign up for an alternate's slot that might open up if someone with an exemption into the field pulled out. By the time everything was settled, he was well down the waiting list, in ninth position. He and Bettye went back to Memphis, not expecting to hear from the tournament, which was being staged outside Indianapolis, Indiana.

Taking a busman's holiday, Daly played twenty-seven holes of golf with friends from Chickasaw Country Club on Monday. Tuesday he did a little something for Bettye. He took her out and bought her a new red BMW, so she'd have a classy car to run around in when she became his wife. Wednesday night they were supposed to have dinner with several other couples, until a call came in at five o'clock. Daly had moved up to first place on the waiting list. The tournament, which was located 450 miles away, started in fifteen hours. If a place became available, Daly would have to be there to be able to accept it. What did he want to do? He said he was coming.

They took the BMW, although its precision German engine wasn't supposed to be run at high rpm for the first few thousand miles. There wasn't any good reason for John Daly to begin reading or following instructions now. Eddie Money and Bad Company and Michael Bolton were on the sound system, turned up loud, with the air conditioner belting out the BTUs and the cruise control taking care of the footwork. The interminable construction on I–57 through Illinois had been completed, and there was nothing to break their stride. The exit signs smeared into a blur until John and Bettye coasted to a halt in Carmel, Indiana. It had been a seven-and-a-half-hour ride, with dinner at McDonald's factored in.

The red message light on their phone at the hotel was glowing as gently as a miniature Christmas tree light. John Daly was going to play in the third major of his career. Perhaps it was fatigue from the drive, but before he went to sleep that night he decided for once that making the cut would be enough. He didn't have to beat the world before he turned twenty-six.

7

Wild Thing

 John and Bettye arrived in Carmel between two storms. The first had dumped an inch of rain on the Crooked Stick Golf Course, the tournament site, on Tuesday. The Midwest had been suffering through a corn-withering drought that summer, and such an insignificant amount of precipitation didn't change the essential character of the golf course. It was still so difficult that most everybody who played a practice round agreed that the best way to describe the layout was by using profanity.

Crooked Stick had been specially prepared for the PGA Championship by Pete Dye, the most sadistic golf course designer in the world. Dye believed that golfers loved the game because it was so fiendishly impossible to master, so he built courses that capitalized on that. He peppered them with huge sand traps, omnipresent water hazards, and acres of irregular playing surfaces. When golfers finished a round on one of his courses, Dye wanted them to sigh in relief. Giving a designer with this mind-set the chance to prepare a course for a major, where the landscape was supposed to make professionals gnash their teeth, was to redefine the word *exacting*.

Dye had stretched the course to a difficult 7,289 yards. It was the second longest in PGA Championship history. Add in the hazards, the traps, and the sliding-board greens, and you had no less a personage than Jack Nicklaus mopping his brow after a practice round. Nicklaus called Crooked Stick the most difficult golf course he had ever played—and he'd played a lot.

John Daly walked to the first tee on Thursday morning without having had the opportunity to play a practice round, so he was blissfully unaware of what he was supposed to be up against. Like a Saturday afternoon duffer trying out a new public course a couple of towns over, he obtained his information about the layout the old-fashioned way. Even though he was in a tournament with a $1.4 million purse and had hired an experienced caddie who knew the course, Daly paused on the way to the tee and asked a local guy where the hardest holes were.

By the time Daly teed off, at 12:58 P.M., the wind was up and the sky was getting black and laden with storm. They sounded the weather-alert warning sirens at 1:45 and suspended play at 2:14. The wind speed passed 50 mph, and then the thunder and lightning and drenching rain came. Sixteen minutes later, Thomas Weaver, a thirty-nine-year-old man from nearby Fisher, Indiana, was making his way home with a friend, having given up on seeing any more of the tournament that day. He was walking along in a parking area with an umbrella in his hand. Then fierce streaks of lightning darted across the sky, followed immediately by thunder. A few yards short of his car, Weaver was struck and killed by lightning.

When the storm passed and the emergency crews drove off for the hospital, the tournament resumed with a decided edge of sadness to it for the remainder of the day. The fairways were sodden, which would steal roll from the ball and make the marathon course play even longer. But some of the tees had been moved up twenty yards Thursday morning, when the PGA took pity on the golfers. The amalgamation of these two factors would benefit long and scattershot hitters. They'd still be long off the tee, but their mishit balls wouldn't run as far into the rough that bordered the fairways. Crooked Stick had become more difficult for most of the field but more vulnerable to a select few. John Daly was in the latter category.

On his first time around the course, Daly carded a 69, putting him two shots off the lead. This finish earned him a trip to the pressroom, where many hundreds of reporters were lusting for fresh material for their PGA Championship coverage. The major tournaments attract four to five times as many journalists as the standard weekly tournaments do, and that means that many of the reporters present at a major are unfamiliar with recent arrivals on the tour. Such was the case with John Daly, so when he finished going over his round, talking about how he had played each hole, someone asked if he had a nickname. "Yeah," he said, "my friends call me Wild Thing."

The reporters snickered. This wasn't the kind of thing you expected to hear in the press tent on the professional golf circuit. Unlike tennis, pro golf had largely remained true to the upper-class roots of the game. While few of the golfers actually came from moneyed or highly educated backgrounds, they had learned to act as if they did. They were rewarded handsomely for this with the money that seemed to grow wild around the PGA Tour, so such behavior was reinforced. Now here was John Daly flaunting his working-class roots, as the British lower classes sometimes do, and that attracted attention.

A few reporters wrote down Daly's nickname, and fewer still actually used it in their stories—if they mentioned Daly at all. Unknowns appear on the leaderboard after the first rounds of major tournaments every year, and they vanish quickly, done in by their paucity of experience in withstanding the pressure of the biggest events in their sport. Reporters know this, so they are blasé when guys like Daly are brought in for interviews. Often the reporters don't even bother to attend the sessions unless they are bored.

With Daly having played most of that year's tournaments on the PGA Tour, and with him being the tour's longest driver, there were sportswriters at Crooked Stick who knew Daly was a hard-working young golfer who hit the ball a long way. Because hardly any of the writers monitored the Sunshine Tour—or took what happened there seriously—almost no one recognized that Daly had won over $300,000 playing golf during the last twenty months, or that he had learned how to play long, sopping courses while in South Africa.

When Crooked Stick was still wet on Friday, Daly put on a driving display that he usually reserved for the practice range. While his longest drives were spectacular to watch, they were immensely difficult to control, so he attempted them only periodically during tournaments. If Daly was swinging with all his might and he wasn't on that day, it was simply too easy to shoot an 85 and miss the cut. In most tournaments, Daly would go broke if he hammered it on every tee.

But he was in the zone at the PGA Championship that Friday, and the course was slow, allowing him to blast one 300-yard drive after another. On the holes on which the players' tee shots were being measured, he was hitting the ball almost twenty yards longer than his normal tour average—and car lengths beyond everyone else. Daly stormed Crooked Stick on Friday with a five-under-par 67, which gave him the tournament lead. Simultaneously, all of the players with marquee value had miserable rounds. Suddenly the good ol' boy from Arkansas was no longer a first-round curiosity item for the media. Now he was the entire story of the tournament.

Daly was brought into the pressroom again, and this time people were fighting for seats. Daly repeated the story of how he almost hadn't made it into the tournament and told them about the long ride from Memphis that he'd made on speculation. He said that, the best he could recall, he thought his longest drive might have been one of 379 yards on the Hogan Tour last year. And yes, he had gone to the University of Arkansas, and he remained a "beloved" fan of the Razorbacks, but that he had left after three years because he got tired of playing golf for free.

On a tour on which many of the young players were frequently accused of being clones spewed out by college golf factories, this guy was irresistible. Not only could he kill the golf ball, he could also aw-shucks you to death in the pressroom. A reporter asked Daly how he was going to handle the pressure of being in the lead. "I'm telling myself it's just another golf tournament," he said. "I'm just going to swing as hard as I can and make birdies."

In his heart of hearts, Daly knew this couldn't really be happening. People had been drumming one point into his head for a half-dozen years: He was only a kid, and kids don't become prominent players—or win majors—on the PGA Tour. It had been a titanic struggle to even begin to accept this notion, which everybody told him he had to embrace before the bitter fires of disappointment consumed his soul. Now fate, and these reporters, were trying to twist his mind around and get him believing in that stuff again, the myth about what it was going to be like—the one that had started to imprint itself on his brain as he'd stood there in knee pants in Wildcat Hollow watching Jack Nicklaus on TV.

Not long after John Daly was in the pressroom, Jim and Lou Daly would return to the very same house in Dardanelle where that dream had begun. There was a new electronic device there now, across from where the TV sat. It was a telephone answering machine, which was loaded with messages. The Dalys had been incommunicado for days, coming back from a vacation in California. They would push the playback button and words would spill into the room from friends and family about the second-round leader of the PGA Championship. This time it wasn't Jack Nicklaus, though; it was their son.

The Dalys debated flying to Indiana for the weekend but decided not to. They didn't want to interfere with John's concentration. There would be other major tournaments, and they would attend those if John wanted them to. If they had asked John about coming, he would have told them to stay home. He was certain the illusion would shatter momentarily. As he told the reporters at his press conference on Friday, sounding as though he didn't expect to see them again, "I'll remember this day for the rest of my life."

After two days of being shown only on cable stations during the daytime, the PGA Championship went network on the weekend. It was a big day for the sports programming division of CBS. Having paid $4 million to win the broadcast rights away from ABC, CBS was going to be presenting the PGA Championship for the first time in twenty-seven years.

There were people at the network who were leery of this tournament, as it was frequently the least exciting major. Yet being a major, they had to pay serious money for it, which required extra hours of coverage to produce a profit. If the tournament was a snooze, remote controls would be blazing throughout the land, and CBS officials would have to swallow hard and smile. All of this became academic when John Daly blew in off the interstate and vaulted into the lead of the PGA Championship.

Gary McCord, a sometimes tour player and regular CBS color commentator, couldn't believe his good fortune in having someone like Daly in the lead to enliven the program. McCord was the Fuzzy Zoeller of the broadcast booth—a funny and highly irreverent man who loved to shoot verbal bullets at people's feet. He also had a fine appreciation of the absurd. When the greens became especially fast at the Masters Tournament, McCord would suggest that the putting surfaces might have been bikini-waxed. The members of the host course would be so aghast that their tournament and pubic hair had been alluded to in the same sentence, they would have McCord banned from future broadcasts of the Masters.

CBS paid McCord to be the only genuine quipster working in golf TV. That was not always an easy calling to fulfill—the people behind the scenes in golf could be as brittle as low-grade glass, and the leaderboard sometimes featured the banal pursuing the meek. After two days of watching John Daly in all of his glorious rawness, McCord put on his headset on Saturday—when the monster audiences would tune in—feeling as if he'd just won the lottery.

John Daly's story of arriving in town twelve hours before his tee time, after being the ninth alternate, and then bulldozing through the field was playing well in the newspapers. But it was television programming worthy of a sweeps period. The sight and sound of TV captured the essence of the Daly story that weekend: this hulking country boy with a paunch, a bad haircut, and a driver like a bazooka, and the fickle galleries, screaming in disbelief at his drives, who came to love him.

Early in the broadcast, CBS presented a graphic comparing the clubs Daly had used on his second shot on each of four holes with those other golfers had used. After ripping the ball off the tee, Daly was often using five clubs less than his competitors to hit to the green. McCord couldn't get enough of it. "He will not back off on the driver," McCord said. "He will take it out on every hole and hit it as hard as he can. I've never seen an exhibition of strength and power overwhelming a course like this."

CBS offset McCord's jazzy informality with the starchy commentary of Ben Wright, an Oxbridge-sounding Brit who believed that excess had no place in life except when one was exhibiting reserve. Yet even Wright was taken by Daly's aplomb. "What a colossal hitter this man is," he said. "I've never seen anything like it. He's not fazed at all by the exalted company, and he's putting on an awesome display. They'll be flocking to see this phenomenon in the months and years to come."

Caught up in the fever, many of the announcers engaged in hyperbole, based on comments Daly had made in the pressroom. They said Daly was able to swing so hard that he exploded golf balls and caved in the face of metal drivers, and that his club moved so fast they couldn't catch it on slow motion. None of that was totally true, but quibbling wasn't in the spirit of the day.

Then, with Daly on the back side of a round in which his lead in the tournament would reach four strokes at one point, the ultimate rendezvous occurred. The fans on the course were cheering so loudly and so often for Daly that they threatened to drown out the on-course announcers, and that was nice. But something of pivotal importance played out when Jack Nicklaus took off his spikes and walked into the broadcast booth to become a commentator. Since Daly was still on the course, it meant that it was Nicklaus's turn to watch Daly play golf on TV.

If Daly had modeled his golf swing on that of Nicklaus, it was the only aspect of Nicklaus's life that he had paid any attention to. Nicklaus had been a golf prodigy whose childhood ascent through the game had been monitored by a doting pharmacist father and a country club golf teacher, who devoted themselves to this boy of great promise. When other children of the 1950s were still trying to decide whether they were going to be a policeman or a fireman, Nicklaus had already decided not simply that he was going to play the PGA Tour but that he was going to be a historic figure in golf. Little Jackie Nicklaus took himself very seriously.

When John Daly was playing badly during a round, he wanted to give up. Nicklaus couldn't wait to get to the practice range to hit balls and consult with others until he had eliminated his swing flaws. Like Daly, Nicklaus had been heavy, but the calories came from ice cream rather than beer. Nicklaus sometimes even smoked cigarettes, like Daly, but he most certainly never teed off with a Marlboro dangling off his lower lip, the way Daly did—during tournaments, no less.

Nicklaus parted company with Daly over form. Nicklaus believed there was a right way and a wrong way to do everything, and he followed the former path exclusively. It wasn't snobbery. Nicklaus was amazingly accessible for so accomplished a man. It was more that he suffered from an overabundance of rationality, whereas Daly was a prisoner of whim.

Nonetheless, both men hit the golf ball a long way and had done so since an early age, and Daly had told everyone who would listen that Nicklaus had been his hero. Nicklaus knew of Daly. People had been talking about his Nicklaus-like length, and Nicklaus had invited Daly to his 1991 Memorial Tournament, held only a few months before. Daly had gone and shot 74, 74, 83, 83—scores that were not uncommon for Daly on a bad week but which were unthinkable to Nicklaus.

With Nicklaus in the broadcast booth at the PGA Championship and Daly leading the tournament, Nicklaus was going to have to go on the record about Daly before the closing credits rolled. Moments after coming into the booth, Nicklaus was asked to analyze a slow-motion video of Daly's swing. "What a coiling, what an unleashing of power," Nicklaus said. "He's obviously doing a lot of things right this week, and I wish him well."

Nicklaus's beliefs and opinions were so strongly held that

he couldn't bluff worth a damn. His fellow broadcasters knew he was dying to counsel Daly. Nicklaus was fifty-one and the father of five grown children. He had won everything there was in golf; he was known around the world; and his Golden Bear International operation had made him rich. By now, Jack Nicklaus was the Godfather of Golf—dispensing unsolicited advice was part of what he did.

Broadcaster Jim Nantz mentioned to Nicklaus that Daly had grown up trying to copy Nicklaus's swing. "I don't think his swing looks very much like mine," Nicklaus said flatly, and there it was on the table. Let's be up-front about this. There was about as much chance that Nicklaus would swing a club back past parallel to the ground at the top of his swing as there was that he would do a triple gainer into a bean field in a Chevy Blazer.

"I like the path of the swing, and I'm sure as John gets a little older it will change a little bit," Nicklaus said, catching himself. He didn't want to be a prig and criticize the kid during his moment of glory. But oh, if only this Daly boy would listen to Jack Nicklaus, think of what he could accomplish. "It will get shorter, as we all do. Right now it's working, so use it and go knock the devil out of the ball."

Nantz mentioned that Daly had said he wasn't feeling any pressure as of Saturday. "He isn't feeling it yet, and I just hope everyone leaves him alone and lets him play. I'm sure he's going to think a little bit tonight. He'll have his problems," Nicklaus said ominously.

Then Nicklaus's iron will broke, and he blurted out: "John Daly is going to have to learn. If he's going to be a good player as well as a long hitter, he's going to have to learn to collect himself and play. . . . I'm sitting here talking. I wish him all the best."

Out on the course, Daly was receiving a very different reception. Walking up the eighteenth fairway with a three-shot lead, he was greeted by the type of thunderous ovation that is usually reserved for the winner of the tournament on Sunday. There were still eighteen holes to go, but the fans didn't care. They adored this man and all of his flagrant quirks. And perhaps they were a bit afraid—afraid that Daly might realize what he was in the middle of and falter. They were telling him it would be okay.

John and Bettye had a big night on Saturday as they began to discover what instant celebrity did for their social life. The Indianapolis Colts football team was playing an exhibition game at the Hoosier Dome, and John and Bettye were invited by the team's owners to be their guests for the evening. The team sent a limo over to bring them to the stadium, and they were ushered up to the luxury box seats.

John said he wanted to go down on the field, and that was okay, but the team was wondering whether he should be introduced over the public-address system. This was a football crowd, and they might not know who John Daly was—as hardly anyone had before the last few days. It would be terribly embarrassing, for all concerned, if no one clapped after his name was called out. He'd be left standing there waving to tens of thousands of blank faces.

The tournament had been all over the sports segment of the local TV newscasts by then, and Daly had been featured prominently in them. The chances were that his notoriety had cross-pollinated to all sports fans by Saturday night—at least in the Indianapolis area. So they gave it a try and introduced him. The stadium exploded with applause.

It was the eighteenth hole all over again. People were shouting and screaming and clapping until their hands hurt. Daly was overjoyed. He was at a National Football League game, and an entire stadiumful of people were cheering for him. They were yelling because a guy who looked just like them—not overly attractive, a bit out of shape, mostly ordinary in every way—could drive a golf ball like a figure out of Greek mythology. Daly ran around and slapped high fives with anyone he could reach. He signed autographs and smiled, all the while absorbing every ounce of adulation his system could endure.

John Madden, the most famous football announcer in America and a no-nonsense guy himself, was broadcasting the football game for CBS. He had a videotape of Daly's swing sent over, and he played it. He drew diagrams and lines over it, the way he did with football plays. Even jaded professional sports people were blubbering about the way John Daly swung a golf club. Never in the history of golf had the third-round leader of a tournament been celebrated like this.

What with all the excitement that night, and the monstrous anticipation of what was to come, Daly drank some beer that evening. He drank to take the edge off. He drank to feel the surge. He drank for extra courage. Ultimately, he drank to forget. By the time Bettye tucked him in, John would be so addled with booze that he would remember little of his moment beneath the lights of the Hoosier Dome. It was safer like that.

Bringing It Home

Gary McCord began to understand that it wasn't only golf nuts, that other people were getting into this, too, when strangers stopped him on the street during the tournament to ask about John Daly. They'd share an observation or ask a question, and many times it would be the big question of the PGA Championship: Was Daly going to fold?

People had been talking during the broadcast about the possibility of a choke because you had to. It was a fact of sports. Golfers who hadn't won a big one yet, and those with weak constitutions, allowed themselves to think about the consequences and implications of what they were caught up in. With everything factored in, a win in a major—especially for a guy like Daly, someone with an outsized persona—could be worth millions. But the Catch–22 was that if you allowed yourself to think about that, you would never be able to win. You'd pull a tee ball or push a putt because it wasn't just another shot anymore, it was your future. No one could calculate cash flow and drop a complex putt simultaneously.

Veteran players who have won majors go into a trance at

times like this. They begin hitting the ball out of instinct and allow themselves to be pulled along by the energy of the crowd. They become part of the spectacle. They are the ones who snatch out the clubs and strike the balls, but it seems to happen involuntarily. Decisions about club selection and the shape of a shot jump out at them as though they were being dictated by the course itself. Doubt and negativity are blocked from their consciousness. It is a given that they will win.

With the sense of identification Daly had forged with his fans, there were people who got heavily invested in the condition of his psyche on Sunday. A guy from Indianapolis named Jeff Hall became so incensed at those who foretold Daly's doom that he decided to go public with his support. After Saturday's round, he called a friend who owned a T-shirt store and ordered two dozen custom shirts. The message he had emblazoned across them was: Daly Believers. As the shirts were being printed, Hall recruited family and friends to accompany him to the course on Sunday, where they became the newest cult in Indiana.

Down in Dardanelle, there was a local tournament scheduled at the Bay Ridge Boat and Golf Club, but they had a TV available in the pro shop for people to watch the PGA Championship. Jim and Lou Daly had the TV on in the family room, waiting for their company to arrive. John's aunt Ann and uncle Ben were driving east from Fort Smith, Arkansas, near the Oklahoma border, and Jim and Lou's friends from Dardanelle, Wanda and Deward Ferguson, were going to stop by. Other people from the area had driven up to the tournament Saturday night. Rick Ross, Daly's teacher and friend, drove all night with a fellow teaching pro to reach Crooked Stick in time for the final round, and other guys had motored up from Memphis.

The man who was the catalyst for all of this activity shook the cobwebs out of his head on Sunday morning and prepared to face the course he had gotten the best of for three days. Before he left the Radisson Hotel, where they were staying, John gave Bettye one mandate. If he won this thing, he told her, she'd better come running out on the eighteenth green after the last putt dropped and throw herself at him in front of the TV cameras. That's what golf wives did when their husbands won, and even though they weren't married yet, he expected husband treatment.

Daly was mobbed the moment he got out of his car at Crooked Stick. He smiled at people and signed autographs with a cigarette stuck in his mouth but kept moving toward the sanctuary of the locker room. It wasn't peaceful there, as guys who had finished the tournament were emptying their lockers and preparing to leave town, and reporters wandered around searching for people they wanted to interview.

An attendant unlocked Daly's locker for him, and he quickly sorted through all the folded papers that had been stuffed into the ventilation louvers in the door. There were the usual announcements from the PGA Tour office about activities and sign-up deadlines relating to coming tournaments. Then Daly came upon something that caught his eye. It seemed to be a personal note on white paper. When he opened it, it read: *John, Go get 'em.* The signature was *Jack Nicklaus.*

Daly smiled and tucked the note carefully into his locker. No question about it—he was going to frame that son of a bitch. But first he had a golf tournament to win—if he could get out of the clubhouse. There was a swarm of people surrounding the front of the building, patiently waiting in the sunny and mild 78-degree weather for their conquering hero to appear. His tee time was a while away, and there were dozens of highly talented golfers on the course right then that they could be watching, but they weren't interested. They wanted to scrutinize John Daly as he walked from the locker room to the practice range so that they could say they'd seen him. The security people, fearing for Daly's safety, faked them out, hustling Daly out a back door and over to the range.

With a three-shot lead, this tournament was Daly's to lose. The course had been playing to his advantage all week, and he needed to build on that. This was the PGA, and other golfers were certain to be shooting robust final rounds. Yet with his lead, Daly would have to play ineptly for them to win. He didn't mean to let that happen.

Daly was intercepted on his way to the first tee by Bobby Clampett, another PGA Tour member who also did time behind a CBS microphone. At thirty-three, Clampett was one of the younger men working in TV golf. He was a serious Christian, a Brigham Young University graduate, and someone who could give the impression at times that he had cornered the world's supply of bliss.

"You have been the figure this week," Clampett said to Daly, "and I've just been happy to be part of it and watch you play. How did you sleep last night?"

"I slept pretty good," Daly said. He had never been flattered or treated this well by so many people before. It felt terrific, and with millions of viewers watching on live TV, Daly decided it was time to start dispensing paybacks.

"I'll tell you what," Daly said. "As good a job as you're doing, Bobby, you might want to give up golf and do this commentating."

Clampett smiled. "How was the Colts game for you?"

"It was great. The people welcomed me," Daly said. Then, remembering how miserable the team's record had been for years, he put a good word in for the coach. "I think Ron Meyer has something up his sleeve on that Colts team."

Daly bogeyed the first hole after playing it safe by hitting a one-iron rather than a driver off the tee. It was a mistake he wouldn't repeat. He kept ripping the ball, but he was only one under par for the round through the front nine. Fortunately, no one was mounting a charge against him. That was good enough to keep Gary McCord juiced. He repeated the apocryphal tales of exploding golf balls and collapsed driver heads, then began forecasting the future.

"In these next three or four holes he can really blow this thing out," he said. "We can really have some fun and watch a man beat up a golf course. What I thought was the hardest golf course I'd ever seen coming in here on Monday and Tuesday."

When Jack Nicklaus came to the booth on Sunday, he was asked if he was surprised that Daly was holding up. "What is that saying about going home with the one that brought you?" Nicklaus asked. "That's what he is doing. He started out with a driver and blasting it, and he's still blasting it. That's his mentality. We were just talking about he hit a driver off of ten, and he doesn't need a driver off of ten. But he played it anyway, and that's why he's ahead."

Jim Nantz mentioned to Nicklaus that on Saturday Nantz had asked Nicklaus if Daly remind him of anyone, and at that time Nicklaus hadn't been able to think of anyone in particular. "But many of us," Nantz said, forcing the issue, "think he reminds a lot of people of a young Jack Nicklaus."

Nicklaus wouldn't budge this time–note on the locker or no note on the locker. He said he and Daly had their hands in the same position at the top of their swings, but that was it. "John has sort of said that he has followed me as he has grown up. I don't think I was ever that long. I don't think I was ever probably that aggressive toward the golf course. I think I learned to manage my game at an earlier age, and I think that was why I was more consistent at a young age."

While the boys were arguing it out in the broadcast booth, the phone was ringing frequently at the Daly homestead in Dardanelle. Some of the calls were from relatives and friends, but a number were from total strangers who, having heard

Dardanelle mentioned on the broadcast, called directory assistance and got the Dalys' number. Mostly they were people calling to offer their best wishes, but one was from a hungry Reebok representative in New York looking to get the inside track. He asked the Dalys to pass along a sponsorship offer to their son.

The final nine holes on Sunday are where tournament leaders get short of breath, and John Daly was no exception. He could do no better than par on the par-five eleventh hole, and he barely made par on the twelfth. Daly picked up his ball from the cup on the twelfth green and headed for the roped-off path to the thirteenth tee, momentarily disappearing from view of the TV cameras. When he reappeared on camera, he was still in the passageway, but he was carrying a large white cup that he hadn't had before. There was an operator there with a portable camera, and he pointed it directly at Daly and his cup. Daly eyed the camera warily as he moved onto the thirteenth tee.

"Having a nice soft drink right there. You've got to wet the whistle, you know," Gary McCord said in his voice-over. The camera operator zoomed in on Daly and his cup, and Daly quickly raised the container to his mouth, burying his nose in it and taking a purposeful and concealing, ten-second nonstop gulp.

"And Ben," McCord said, speaking to Ben Wright, "I think we'll take it over to you and you can bring him in on this hole."

"Well, I—" Wright began, then stuttered, his voice so swollen with disbelief that he could barely get the words out, "I-I have a feeling that's a beer."

John Daly had pulled world-class stunts before in his life, but if he was drinking an alcoholic beverage during a professional golf tournament, his audacity exceeded his length off the tee by miles. It would be like a boxer popping an amphetamine in his corner between rounds of a championship fight. Short of cheating, it would be hard to imagine a more flagrant violation of the rules. Recognizing that, Ben Wright hurried on with his commentary, talking about another golfer.

Daly birdied the next hole, dropping a difficult twenty-foot putt, then reappeared on-screen with the white cup. Wright granted him a reprieve. "He now has a five-stroke lead after that silky putt. He is a phenomenon. I think he deserves a little sip of the real thing."

That five-stroke lead was diminished by two after the inevitable double bogey Daly scored on the seventeenth hole. As he walked up the eighteenth fairway, with a comfortable, impressive, and winning lead, the tournament, and all of golfdom, was his. Chills engulfed him as he egged his already ecstatic gallery on to even greater volume by giving them an Arsenio Hall rolling-fist salute. He waved and blew kisses to them. Their ovation became deafening as he neared the green.

Bettye came charging across the putting surface, on cue, wearing a black floral-print outfit and especially large sunglasses. John buried his face in her hair to regain his composure as Jim Nantz approached with a microphone. Nantz congratulated Daly, and as John spoke, his voice was heavy and cracking. His accent, barely noticeable most of the time, was suddenly as thick as the syrup at the Waffle House on a cold day.

"I just want to say hi to my mom and dad, and I love them," Daly said. "Chickasaw, and these fans, I won it for y'all. And for this beautiful woman here."

"John's fiancée, Bettye," Nantz said, not using her last name. "They'll be getting married on October eighth."

"Your name is going to be engraved on a trophy that includes the names of Gene Sarazen, Walter Hagen, who won this trophy five times, and Jack Nicklaus," Nantz said. "John Daly's name will be right there."

"I tell you, I love Jack Nicklaus. He's been my idol ever

since. I'm looking at his name right now," Daly said. He looked at the camera and called out: "I love you, Jack."

Down in Dardanelle, Jim and Lou had jumped up to embrace each other when John sank his final putt. When he mentioned his parents during the trophy presentation, they cried. As the broadcast ended and John went to his press conference, Jim turned to the small group of people sitting in his family room. "Everybody doesn't have a son that does something like this," he said. "I guess we did the right thing, taking him around when he was young and moving where there were golf courses to play on."

As John slid behind the table at the front of the pressroom, someone handed him a beer to cool off with, and he took it gratefully. He talked about his round and about how he had fed off the electricity generated by the fans. But even with all of his fan support, he said, he had done it his way. He said he could be stubborn and didn't take to teaching too good. Ultimately, he said, he had "no one to blame for this win but me, and I love it."

A reporter asked Daly how he felt about becoming an overnight celebrity. "I love every minute of it," he said. "It is the greatest thing that ever happened to me."

Someone asked how to spell Bettye's last name, and Daly said not to worry about it, to just make it the same as his because it would be that in the near future. He said he would play in Vegas in October and "take some of the money and maybe play a little blackjack. The marriage will be first, though. October eighth, in Las Vegas."

Asked how he was going to spend the $230,000 he had just won, Daly said that he was going to pay off his house and Bettye's BMW. "I don't know what you guys' favorite charity is here in Indianapolis," he said, "but I'm giving $30,000 to it. The fans won this tournament for me. This is a miracle. Things like this just don't happen."

In the back of the room, Bettye was holding a miniature

press conference of her own. She told reporters who weren't based in the South that her name was Fulford and that she was thirty. John's drinking problem was an open secret among tour players by now but hadn't been written about in national publications, and so when Bettye was asked if John drank, she put a positive spin on things. She said that John "liked to have a good time and, yes, he liked to drink. But he's really settled down in the last year." There was a side of John that other people didn't see, she said, and that was that "he is a nice, generous person."

Daly broke away from the press conference so he could meet with his buddies from home in the clubhouse. Everyone was cruising on adrenaline and raw excitement, lost in the congratulatory stage of the celebration. The guys told Daly how well he had done and how proud they were of him, until even he got sick of it. Then people started ticking off the ways in which Daly's life was going to be different.

His victory gave him a ten-year exemption on the PGA Tour, exemptions into the other major tournaments, and entry into a slew of end-of-the-year, made-for-TV golf matches where the cups on the greens seemed to be crammed with thousand-dollar bills. This was the money he'd actually have to compete for, which would be greatly overshadowed by the money people would throw at him if he was managed properly. Reebok had a $400,000-plus-bonuses offer in the works; Wilson Sporting Goods, which made a hundred million golf balls a year in Tennessee, was working up something bigger. Offers of appearance fees for playing in foreign tournaments and corporate events were being mulled over.

A PGA of America official who arrived to escort John and Bettye to the champion's dinner overheard the conversation. He said he thought he could resolve the debate for them. Their educated guess, the man said, was that winning a PGA Championship was worth $12 million in additional income over the course of someone's career. Everyone stood there for a minute trying to comprehend $12 million. They couldn't, so they let the whole idea go.

John and Bettye had to attend the dinner, but the boys from home started patching together a postmeal celebration for John, Dardanelle style. First they hired a limousine, because that was how you signified something important was going on. It would be one with a moon roof, so John could pop it back and stick his head out and wave to people while they were riding around, if he wanted to. They'd buy an ample supply of beer. Maybe hang out at the hotel for a while, as if it were any other night. You knew John wasn't going to be putting on any airs. When John got hungry, as he always did, they'd pile into the limo and make a McDonald's run. It would be a blast.

Except when things got going at the hotel, there were all of these interruptions. Ron Meyer, the coach of the Indianapolis Colts, came by. He had been at the course on Sunday and saw the reaction Daly provoked from golf fans—it was the same as at the Hoosier Dome on Saturday night. With the Colts, who hadn't played well since moving to Indianapolis, being 0–2 in the preseason, Meyer's team wasn't providing a lot of excitement for its fans. Another preseason home game was scheduled the following Saturday, and Meyer had what he thought was a terrific idea.

Daly had told Meyer on Saturday night that he had been the star kicker for the Helias Crusaders in high school, and now Meyer wanted him to reprise that role—in the National Football League. Against snorting, snot-spewing, three-hundred-pound defensive players who charged kickers with the demeanor the bull presents to the matador. These were guys who hurt people for a living. After Daly had just been told that he would earn an additional—not total, additional—$12 million in his golf career.

Meyer said it would be for only one week, as the backup, kicking one extra point, and only if Daly missed the cut at the tournament he was playing in Colorado. Think, he pitched, of the pregame publicity, the frenzy at the stadium when the words from the public address system reverberated through the stadium: *Now kicking for the Indianapolis Colts . . . John Daly.*

Daly was insane for the idea, but he had to allow that he was a bit worried about getting hurt. What with his having a pretty good future in golf and all. No problem, Meyer said; we'll just tell the opposing team, the one that will be trying to demolish our side the other fifty-nine minutes of the game, to kind of hold back a little on this one play, even though we'd get a point if you make it. They'd probably do it. I mean, what the heck, right?

Daly talked it over with his agent, and they reached a unanimous decision—Hell, yes! He was the PGA Champion. He was invincible.

9

Details

It was 4 A.M. Monday by the time the boys all cleared out of John and Bettye's hotel. John's wake-up call came an hour later. He would be appearing on the CBS program *Good Morning America,* from a set that had been assembled on the eighteenth green at Crooked Stick. Johnny Carson's office had called about a possible appearance on the *Tonight Show.* A *Larry King Live* spot on CNN was confirmed. A *Sports Illustrated* cover story was being written. *People* magazine would be doing a piece. Governor Bill Clinton declared Monday to be John Daly Day in Arkansas. The *Washington Post,* the *Chicago Tribune,* the Memphis *Commercial Appeal,* and the Arkansas papers were all preparing editorials praising Daly and his unforeseen victory. *Time* magazine was doing a story with an illustration showing how Daly's backswing varied from the norm. An invitation from the White House was in the works.

Amid this agreeable onslaught, Daly was in no shape to drive nine hundred miles to his next tournament, the International, which was being staged south of Denver at Castle Rock, Colorado. He and Bettye left the BMW in Indiana and flew west. John had committed to play the tournament, and he didn't want to back out. His life had become like that of a skier who hears an avalanche breaking loose behind him: If he stopped to look back, he would be pummeled. His only option, after all the years of work and dreams, was to grin and keep poling.

John and Bettye got haircuts together in Colorado on Tuesday morning at Fantastic Sam's, an inexpensive hair-salon chain. Tuesday afternoon they had planned to take a sightseeing trip into the nearby Rocky Mountains, but there was an incident at their hotel. Bettye suffered a shoulder separation and had to get medical treatment. She said she tripped over a table while running to answer the phone. She had to have her arm put in a sling.

John was stopped by the police as he was driving from their hotel to the course on Wednesday morning, and he got kind of nervous for a minute. But it wasn't anything. The cops just wanted an autograph from the new PGA champion.

On Thursday, the Tyson chicken family of Arkansas flew Jim and Lou Daly, and Rick Ross, to Castle Rock on one of their corporate jets and put them up, so they could watch John play. Or at least try to watch him play. When the hype about John's length from Crooked Stick was combined with the knowledge that the thin air in the Rockies allows struck balls to travel 10 to 15 percent farther than at sea level, people were running around the Castle Pines Golf Club like it was the second coming. They were practically stampeding from hole to hole. The hottest live sex show imaginable wouldn't have drawn more people than Daly did at the practice range. On the long downhill holes on the course, if John really cranked it, his ball flight was ludicrous.

When Jim Daly came out to the course to watch John on Friday, there was a swarm of people around the first tee waiting for John to start his round. Jim Daly walked up behind them and called out: "Careful what you say, now, that's my son up there." Hardly anybody could resist turning around to look at Jim, and a number of people said hello to him and congratulated him on John's accomplishments.

It was impossible for anyone to really know what John Daly was going through, having all of this notoriety thrust on him ten years before everybody told him it would happen. A reporter asked Daly at a press conference if he was intimidated by the expectations that came with all the attention. "A week ago, nobody had any expectations for John Daly," he said with an unanticipated sharpness. "My expectations are inside myself. My expectations for me are the same as they've always been. They're my own; inside me."

Daly started off well in the tournament, which uses an unconventional scoring system that encourages golfers to gamble and shoot for the flag—just John Daly's brand of golf. At least it was until the third round, on Saturday. He was tired, and although he had gotten plenty of sleep during the week, he didn't feel rested. He seemed to lose all interest in the tournament, and on two holes he got so disgusted with his play that he picked up his ball and walked off the green without putting out. In a normal tournament, he would have been disqualified. At the International, the only consequence was a bad enough score to assure that Daly wouldn't make the cut at the end of the day, which appeared to be his purpose.

The substitute-kicker gig with the Indianapolis Colts had fallen through, so Daly didn't have to dash to catch a flight to Indianapolis. It turned out that nobody other than the coach, Daly, and Daly's agent thought this was a good idea. The Colts' regular kicker asked if he was going to get a shot at the PGA Tour. The guy who held the ball for the kicker refused to hold for Daly, saying he didn't want to get his fingers kicked off by an amateur. The general manager, realizing the stunt would never be approved by the league office, had killed it, saying it wasn't a good idea to put the future Jack Nicklaus at risk.

Daly was not without other opportunities for diversion, however. The Colts deal was replaced by an offer from the Denver Broncos football team to come kick field goals at their practice session on Sunday morning, which Daly accepted gleefully. This came after CBS Sports took Daly out to an airport and videotaped him hitting drives on a concrete runway where, between the thin air and the hard surface, the ball seemed as though it might bounce to infinity. Actually, it stopped after 800 yards. At night, when the games were over, there were five times more invitations to socialize than John and Bettye could accept—many from notable people who wouldn't have extended such offers two weeks earlier.

Although Bettye had spent almost all of her time with John on the road, she didn't like the changes that began to occur as soon as his ball rattled in the eighteenth cup at the PGA on Sunday. The people rushing to get to John sometimes elbowed Bettye out of the way—as though she was nobody, as though she wasn't the shepherd of his success—and she didn't cotton to that. Too often the new fans were young women. Bettye quickly grew weary of the competitive pressures of their new rock-star lifestyle.

One evening Bettye went to Rick Ross, John's teacher and friend, in an agitated state. She said she wanted John back for herself. She said she couldn't keep up with him and the glitter crowd any longer, but she didn't want to lose him. She asked Ross what she could do to save their relationship.

Ross was surprised by this, as John still spoke of Bettye as his fiancée. He seemed as eager as ever to marry her in Vegas in October, as planned. "Bettye," Ross said, "you're on the fastest train in the world right now. A lot of people live for this opportunity. You're either going to have to get off and wait for John to get off when it stops, or you're going to have to stay on with him. You have to make a choice. If you try to do it halfway, your relationship will become even more unstable than you think it is now."

Bettye said she would try to stay with John, but she wasn't sure how long she could hang on. She said she didn't think she could take more than a couple of weeks of constantly trying to compete with all of these important people for John's attention. More than anything, she said, she didn't want them to take John away from her.

After the International, John and Bettye flew to Portland, Oregon, for a quick pro-am tournament, and then on to Akron, Ohio. John was playing in the World Series of Golf there, an invitational tournament that is restricted to players who have won recently. Befitting Daly's new status, a PGA Tour staff member had driven Bettye's red BMW over from Indianapolis, and it was waiting at the tournament. Also awaiting Daly's arrival were gangs of fans, and they had only one thing on their minds. They wanted to see this boy nail a golf ball.

The courses at Firestone Country Club, site of the World Series, are notorious for their narrow, tree-lined fairways. The only way a golfer can be in contention there is if he plays smart, precision golf: frequently substituting irons for woods off the tee, and laying up safe rather than shooting for the flag. If Daly wasn't in the zone—a place he was likely to be only occasionally—he would face two choices every time he played in his post–PGA Championship incarnation. He could play smart and perhaps finish well, or he could smash golf balls and probably score badly but feast on the adulation of thousands of jubilant fans.

At the end of the first round in Akron, Daly was ten over par and fourteen shots off the lead, having put his ball into the fairway off the tee only twice. Nobody cared as long as he signed the programs, visors, jagged pieces of paper, and anything else that would retain ink, that they pushed at him. They also wanted him to hit the driver at least sometimes on the course, and always on the driving range. Daly did that, and people went home happy in Akron, feeling entitled to pepper their conversations over the coming weeks with references to the Babe Ruth of golf.

As it happened, Daly was also going home happy. He'd made the cut and finished fortieth in the tournament before he and Bettye packed the BMW and headed south by southwest. Daly needed a break—although it probably wouldn't end up being that much of a rest, because another dream was about to come true. After having returned to Dardanelle more than once with his tail between his legs—or being towed by a wrecker—Daly was about to be figuratively met at the border and lifted onto the shoulders of the town. The Dardanelle Chamber of Commerce had declared the following Friday to be John Daly Day. They were having a celebration out at the Bay Ridge Boat and Golf Club, and the whole damn town was invited.

People started arriving for the festivities late in the afternoon on Friday, even though the ceremony wouldn't start until 5 P.M., allowing folks to come by after work. The Dardanelle police went to Wildcat Hollow to give Jim and Lou an escort. When they were ready, the Dalys climbed into their pickup and the police flipped on their lights, and the vehicles eased out onto Route 22 for the one-mile trip to Bay Ridge.

Governor Bill Clinton sent an aide, Field Wasson, with a letter of congratulations and a state flag. The speaker of the state House of Representatives came, along with Dardanelle's state senator and representative and the mayor. Mostly, though, the crowd of three hundred was composed of the ordinary citizens of this modest hamlet. They were there because the younger Daly boy had done something thoroughly commendable. Thanks to him, people all over the world had now heard of Dardanelle, Arkansas. His neighbors were there to show their appreciation for that.

A hat was passed, and $400 was collected to erect a sign at Bay Ridge identifying it as the home of John Daly, 1991 PGA Champion. It was mostly locals who played there, so the sign was as much for John to see when he came home as anything. John's friend Kevin Ryals, a country singer from town, performed a song he had written for the occasion, called "Long John Daly." It told the saga of a baby-faced boy who was a monster on the greens.

The officials had their say, before John got up and discovered a tenth of Dardanelle staring at him, waiting for him to speak. He thanked his parents. Don Cline from the hospital was in the audience, and John choked up when he admitted that he had frequently been in trouble in high school and college, and Cline had been like a second father to him at those times. "I want to tell you, Don Cline," he said, "I love you."

Daly nodded to Rick Ross and struggled to say that Ross was one of the best teachers in the world and that he was "one of the biggest reasons my success is the way it is."

Sweeping his eyes over the audience, Daly continued, his voice cracking, "Dardanelle is in this big heart of mine for as long as I ever live. Here I am, twenty-five years old, and it's just like the greatest feeling in the world to know I've got friends and family like you. I just want to keep Dardanelle on the map forever and ever. And I ain't afraid to cry, either."

The emotion in the air was as drenching as the August humidity, and it seemed to wash unpleasant things from people's memories. They were replaced by the entirely new world of possibilities that John Daly's victory had created for so many people. The folks at the Chenal Country Club in Little Rock, whom Daly had been pestering unsuccessfully for a sponsorship, were now prepared to offer him a course-side lot, a club membership, and carte blanche on anything he wanted from the pro shop—balls, tees, spikes, you name it.

Bill Woodley, the reform-minded golf coach at the University of Arkansas who had clashed with Daly so pointedly, could hardly remember what that silliness had been about. My goodness, let bygones be bygones. He would be hosting Daly on Saturday at the nationally televised Arkansas-Miami football game, where Daly was going to be introduced to a packed stadium of Razorback fans at halftime as the university's most recent conquering hero.

Even Bettye Fulford, the woman John had won the PGA Championship for, was caught up in the spirit of reformation. A few hours before the ceremony began in Dardanelle, Bettye's lawyer had quietly filed papers in Bibb County, Georgia, seeking to end her five-year marriage to one Michael Blackshear. Although Bettye had been separated from her husband for two years, she wasn't divorced—a detail she had never apprised John of. Something else would happen with Bettye that she wouldn't tell John about for months. Within days, she would be pregnant.

There were other, more discomfiting particulars of Bettye's past that she had chosen not to share with John, but these matters were out of her control now. All of that information began working its way to the surface the moment Bettye ran across the eighteenth green at Crooked Stick, trying to please John while simultaneously but futilely hoping no one in a national TV audience of 5.5 million would recognize her. As John Daly was becoming a folk hero, his years of assiduous toil rewarded, telephone lines were sizzling throughout the South, echoing with the refrain of disbelief: "Did you see who that was?"

People who recognized Bettye began calling each other, and then they called the PGA Tour office, John's friends, or those who they thought might have once met John's friends. There were more than a few people predisposed to rat Bettye Fulford out. As this telephone tree blossomed, John was drinking heavily from the chalice of fame, blissfully unaware of the hushed but heated talk that was snaking its way inexorably toward him.

Some of the calls came to Rick Ross, who had been identified as Daly's teacher in newspaper stories published in the days after Crooked Stick. Ross heard from people in Georgia, Tennessee, and South Carolina. The first call took his breath away. It came from a couple, one on the upstairs extension, the other in the kitchen, who identified themselves as friends of Bettye—and her husband.

"Husband?" Ross nearly screamed. "What are you talking about, husband?" The couple said if Ross didn't know about Bettye's husband, he must not know about her son, either.

"Son?" Ross asked. "What son?" The couple said he was the son from her first marriage. "First marriage?"

The callers told Ross that Bettye had a thirteen-year-old son from her first marriage and that she was still married to her second husband, Michael Blackshear. They said the boy lived about fifty miles north of Atlanta. They offered to send a picture of him if Ross doubted them. Ross knew people didn't go to all this trouble to lie. He tried to work the numbers, but he was too dazed to do the math on Bettye's age. "Forget the picture," he said. "Tell me how old she is."

They said Bettye was thirty-nine years old, which made her eight years older than she had claimed and fourteen years older than John. Ross thanked the callers and began checking with John's other friends. They too were getting phone calls, or hearing things secondhand, and there was a consistency to the information. The message was: The woman John Daly is desperately in love with, and whom he wants to marry, has badly misrepresented herself to him.

The consensus among Daly's friends was that short of having his PGA Championship trophy revoked on a technicality, this was the worst thing that could happen to him.

Everything good in his career—which was to say his life—had occurred while he was with Bettye. He would explode at this news, feeling a mammoth sense of betrayal. For a man who was predisposed to believe the world was against him, here was confirmation in spades.

For those of Daly's friends who had never liked Bettye—a sentiment mostly reciprocated by her—this was the evidence they needed to support their original hypothesis. Sensing a cool remoteness in her from the beginning, they believed she was an aging ex-cheerleader who hadn't had the easiest of lives and who was determined to get herself a ticket in the first-class section before the last of her beauty faded. Or, as they said to each other out of John's hearing: "That bitch is a gold digger."

When Daly's friends came to him with the news, he responded as if it were a hand grenade that had been tossed at his feet. He grabbed it and threw it back. No way could that be true, he insisted. She wouldn't do that to him. If it were true, why had these people waited until now to come forward? How could Daly not know about it if she had a child?

Bettye joined the chorus instantaneously, swearing to God that none of it was true, not a word of it, it was a pack of damnable lies . . . except possibly, maybe, there might be an outside chance that she was still married. But if it were true, and she wasn't saying that it was, it would only be because she had forgotten to get a divorce. Then she must have forgotten that she'd forgotten. She was almost sure that she was divorced, though, and she was going to check into it and get it straightened out right away. Nonetheless, there was no other marriage and no son, and she was most certainly not thirty-nine years old.

Bettye also launched a fierce counteroffensive, telling John that if these people were his friends, how could they lie to him this way during his moment of triumph? There could be only one reason, and that was because they were trying to end Bettye's relationship with John, as they had been doing since the beginning. These people, who claimed to be his friends, had almost allowed him to drink himself into oblivion. *She* was the one who came along and gave him priorities, not them. *She* was the one who helped make him a champion.

John and Bettye went into seclusion in Memphis, trying to sort things out. Reporters, unaware of the imbroglio on the domestic front, called to inquire how Daly was holding up under all of the post–PGA Championship attention. He told Jaime Diaz of the *New York Times* that his vacation had turned out to be a nightmare. "I just never realized," he said, "what it's like when you go to gas stations and grocery stores and people know who you are. I haven't been left alone by anybody." Daly also said that he was postponing the October eighth wedding—because he was too busy.

Actually, Daly wasn't busy at all, having played only one tournament during September, plus a benefit at Helias High School, where he raised $23,000. At the end of the month, with nothing resolved in his personal life, Daly decided that the best way to deal with his problems was to go play golf every week and try not to think about them. It was an approach that was reminiscent of the program to control alcoholism through tennis.

As John and Bettye were leaving Memphis, Bobby Hall of the *Commercial Appeal* caught up with them. Daly told Hall that taking so much time off was a mistake that he wasn't going to make again. Then, seemingly apropos of nothing, Bettye said: "I've known John for a year and a half. He asked me to quit my job and travel with him on tour. I knew him when he was flat broke, so I'm not out for the money."

Then Bettye and John disappeared on a blitz that included Georgia, Texas, Nevada, Washington, D.C., Arizona, and North Carolina, where he finished third in the Tour Championship in November. This event was restricted to the year's top money-winners and was played on a layout that required delicate shots and clear thinking. Daly showed once again that he was an enormous talent on the course. Off the course, he had gained thirteen pounds since the trouble started two months earlier.

Another stop on this marathon was Carmel, Indiana, where Daly returned to sign lithographs entitled "The Cinderella Story" that commemorated his PGA Championship. He and Bettye also looked at a house and a building lot that was for sale in the area—even though they had been living near Memphis for less than a year. Bettye was pushing for the move, and she talked John into buying the building site. She was dying to get out of Memphis, and John told his buddies that he thought it was because she wanted to get him away from the guys at the Chickasaw Country Club, where he had been given a membership after he won the PGA Championship.

John's buddies weren't overly concerned about Bettye's actions, as unbeknownst to John or Bettye, they had enlisted some of the finest investigators in the South to discover everything there was to know about Bettye Fulford's past.

The Suits

The intensity of the locker-room gossip about John Daly's drinking rose throughout the fall on the PGA Tour, and soon it was augmented by complaints about his behavior at tournaments. Players griped to each other, and to reporters off the record, that Daly had become such a hot dog and a slave to his galleries that he ignored the most basic courtesies due to other golfers. Daly replied, on the record, that some players spent more time worrying about what he was doing than they did about themselves, and that they were only jealous over the tide of attention and opportunities that washed over him every day.

A case in point was the U.S. Skins Game, where four players compete in late November over eighteen holes for more than $500,000 and enough automobiles to fill a new-car–transport truck. Being asked to compete was a coveted financial bonanza. Since this was a made-for-TV event in which golfers were miked, invitations had as much to do with audience appeal as they did with golfing skills. In 1991 John Daly became the first rookie ever to participate in a Skins Game in the United States.

He arrived in California for the event after tournaments in Hawaii and Japan, and met his parents and a friend whom Daly had flown in. He then proceded to upstage veteran golfers Curtis Strange, Payne Stewart, and Jack Nicklaus on the driving range and on the course. He won a record-tying $120,000 on the first nine holes, plus two new cars. The crowd was so blatantly biased toward Daly that Nicklaus told reporters, "This young man has sort of stolen the show." ABC also credited Daly's appearance for the near-record TV audience that watched the first nine holes on Saturday.

If the crowds grew ever more captivated with Daly, Jack Nicklaus remained firm in two beliefs: that Daly had incredible talent, and that he desperately needed guidance. Nicklaus had reached out to Daly after Crooked Stick but had been rebuffed. Very quietly, Nicklaus took Daly aside at the Skins Game and invited him to visit Nicklaus in North Palm Beach, Florida. There were few people in the golf world that Nicklaus was close to, making this an uncommon gesture on his part. This time Daly agreed to come. A date was set for mid-December, after he and Bettye returned from a one-week trip to Sun City, in South Africa, for a tournament called the Million Dollar Challenge.

Sun City is an opulent resort and casino complex located in the black homeland of Bophuthatswana. The compound is situated in the crater of an ancient volcano, a hundred miles northwest of Johannesburg, and it features a large casino, entertainment such as stage shows and nude revues, a wildlife preserve, and a 7,665-yard golf course designed by Gary Player.

Sol Kerzner, the owner of the complex, staged a big-time golf tournament there every year, with a purse equivalent to those of the regular tournaments in Europe. This wasn't one of the training tournaments of the Sunshine Tour; it was meant to attract players with name recognition. Even though the money was competitive, Kerzner began having difficulty attracting top-name golfers because of the political boycott of South Africa in the 1980s.

As a wealthy man, Kerzner knew the riveting effect large sums of money, especially when paid in one chunk, had on people's minds, and the transforming effect it could have on their principles. Kerzner decided to reformat his tournament in 1987, restricting the field to a handful of golfers but offering a first-place prize of $1 million—far exceeding the top prize in any other event. The remainder of the golfers would be paid enough to make it worth their while, but to keep things interesting, it would be a pittance compared to first place. Kerzner was spending his own money here, and he didn't want to see anybody walking off with $1 million without first having spilled blood on his golf course.

Kerzner's scheme worked bit by bit, especially as the political situation changed in South Africa and playing there began to lose its stigma. By the time John Daly arrived in December 1991, the field was composed of ten of the top golfers in the world, and the total purse was $2.5 million. First place still paid $1 million; last place was $100,000.

Daly was never a factor in the 1991 tournament, finishing tied for fifth the first day and deteriorating from there. That was partly because Bernhard Langer, the German golfer, set or tied five records in winning, and partly because Daly didn't play well. Daly ultimately finished eighth, twenty-two shots off the lead, winning $120,000—or at least he won that much in theory.

While in Sun City, Daly went on what had become one of his uniquely traditional gay and carefree South African nights on the town. First he drank, then he gambled and lost heavily, then he returned to his hotel room and proceeded to decimating it. Published reports said Daly might have lost as much as $150,000—giving him a net loss of $30,000 for the week.

John and Bettye returned to the United States for a brief rest before they had to go to Jamaica for John's final tournament of the year. When they arrived in Memphis, John's friends presented him with an early Christmas gift: a six-inch-thick portfolio of documents and investigators' reports that substantiated all of the claims that had been made against Bettye—and more. John told Bettye to call Jack Nicklaus and cancel their planned visit, then he sat down and spent three days going through the dossier.

As John confronted her with each piece of evidence, Bettye insisted it was bogus or that the people who had compiled the material were lying. She admitted to nothing other than her marriage to Michael Blackshear. She continued to maintain that she was thirty-one, even after John produced a yearbook with her picture indicating she had graduated from high school when John was four. There was a lot of shouting, but the increased volume of the discussion didn't raise its lucidity.

After having successfully blocked out what his friends had told him for months, John couldn't persist with the denial any longer. He had lived with this woman for almost eighteen months, traveling all over the world with her and buying her a luxury car, jewelry, and endless gifts with his trademark generosity. He loved her deeply. Now he was feeling grievously deceived—as though he had been played for a fool. That was the worst part—dealing with the paralyzing idea that she had never really loved him, that it was all a scam. When Bettye continued to lie even as John stuck the evidence in her face, what else could he think?

With his head reeling with images of Bettye's duplicity, John had to leave to play golf in Jamaica. He was very close to losing control, but he tried to be decent. He told Bettye that it would be best if she stayed behind in Memphis. She refused. John said he needed some time to think and breathe and figure out how he felt about all of this. Bettye said she wouldn't stay home, that it was important for them to be together at a time like this so she could show him how much she really loved him, and that it was his friends who were the deceivers. John let her come.

The Jamaica tournament was another cash-spewing end-of-the-year made-for-TV special, this time called the World Championship of Golf. The purse was $2.55 million, and just like the Skins Game, no one had any delusions about its being anything other than a profit-making opportunity for everyone involved. Nonetheless, the golfers' total paychecks were tied to their order of finish, so they at least had to make some effort—something they forgot to tell John Daly.

When he stopped fighting with Bettye long enough to go to the golf course, Daly played golf like a man with a lot on his mind. He shot a 77 during the first round and a laughable 87 during a second round in which he snapped his putter in half in anger after four-putting the twelfth hole. On the final six holes, he improvised putting instruments on the greens. He was so far out of the running that he had no real chance of materially improving his position during the final two rounds. In all likelihood he would finish last, but he could take comfort in the $50,000 he would receive as a consolation prize.

Since it was only a twenty-six-man field, there was no two-day cut. With a $50,000 minimum guaranteed, everybody was expected to play four days of golf to earn their checks. Daly was in for a long weekend—until a convenient incident occurred as he was finishing up on Friday. After taking six strokes on the eighteenth hole, Daly signed a scorecard saying he had a five on the hole. The tournament's organizers were forced to disqualify Daly for signing an incorrect scorecard. At the same time, they were obligated to give him the $50,000 last-place paycheck he probably would have earned anyway.

As Daly's three-month blitz of tournament play came to an end, he told sportswriters in Jamaica that he was burned out and that he shouldn't have been there that week. "I should be home," he said. "I just don't feel like playing golf." After having left Tennessee three months earlier in the hope that a major impediment in his relationship would resolve itself in his absence, Daly was about to go home and discover the obstruction had festered so badly it had to be lanced.

John and Bettye were still fighting when they got back to Memphis, but John had pretty much made up his mind that it was time to move on. He told Bettye at Christmas that he was going to Dardanelle to see his parents and he wanted her to clear out while he was gone. He said she could keep the car and the other stuff he had bought her, but it was over. Bettye said that he couldn't do this to her at a time like this. When John asked what that meant, Bettye announced that she was almost four months pregnant with John's baby.

With all the crap that had just come down, John said he wasn't going to believe that unless he saw some baby papers from the doctor. He left to visit with his parents and friends in Dardanelle, and when he returned to Tennessee, Bettye was gone. As he looked around the house, he also discovered that a photo album from the PGA Championship seemed to be missing. A chorus of his friends singing "She's only out for what she can get" reverberated in his mind. He called a locksmith and purchased a sophisticated burglar alarm that would notify the police if anyone tried to enter the house.

As the tradesmen were sweating with hammers and screwdrivers to secure Daly's home in Cordova against Bettye Fulford, she was flying to Los Angeles. She was a woman who was almost forty years old, who was carrying the child of the hottest man in professional golf in her womb. The last time she had checked before she left the house in Cordova, Daly had over $800,000 in cash sitting in various bank accounts, and enough contracts signed to insure that bankers would be sucking up to him for years to come.

Bettye understood in a way that John could not that this

wasn't the Macon Open or the Wildcat Hollow Driving Range anymore. She also knew that she wasn't going back to an existence where making a pedestrian living depended on being able to push the deluxe lunch option on the next realtor's convention she booked into the Madison Room of some Radisson Hotel. Bettye stayed in hotels now; she didn't work in them. When John thought $10-an-hour blue-collar workers could protect him from Bettye, he showed that he was the rube in this battle. Bettye went straight to Marvin Mitchelson.

Mitchelson was the infamous palimony attorney who specialized—quite successfully—in winning settlements for women who had been jilted by wealthy men they had lived with but hadn't married. In the years since Mitchelson had won a high-profile case against the actor Lee Marvin, forty-three states had come to recognize some form of palimony suit, although Tennessee wasn't one of them.

There was also the delicate matter of Fulford's concealed marriage. Mitchelson told Bettye not to worry about these details when she came to see him. He said the aim in these cases wasn't to go to court. The plan was to frighten the man so badly that he would reach for his checkbook out of the fear of going to court. Mitchelson's strategy was to hold the threat of negative publicity over Daly's head and leverage a settlement. Mitchelson was aware that no organization in sports was more image-conscious than the PGA Tour. He was betting that now that Daly was a millionaire, he would have people in his employ who would stress the importance of his public image to him and who would explain the kind of life changes his new wealth was going to necessitate in matters such as these.

With increasing frequency, there would be times in Daly's life when he would have to part with money to make unpleasant things go away. He would pay people who wore expensive suits and delicate shoes to come together with similarly attired people from the other side in rooms with Oriental rugs and indirect lighting. They would threaten each other, bluff, challenge, and then agree upon how much it was going to cost Daly. He would pay because he would be too busy making money to do otherwise.

What Mitchelson utterly failed to factor into this equation was the truckload of emotional baggage John Daly brought to this matter. His friends had been telling him from the beginning that Bettye was in it for the money—which meant she had never loved him. He started to believe them when he discovered Bettye had lied to him about herself. Any lingering doubt he'd had disappeared when Bettye went directly from Daly's house to Marvin Mitchelson's office. To John Daly's mind, there was only one reason women went to men like Marvin Mitchelson. It was because they had never loved the men they had been with.

Mitchelson was right about one thing. Daly did retain people to advise him. Except this time it was Daly who gave them the instructions. They were precise and circumscribed. Regardless of what they had to do, Bettye wasn't to get anything. On December 31, when other men were preparing for a night on the town with their women to celebrate the coming of the new year, John Daly made a phone call to the offices of the PGA Tour near Jacksonville, Florida. He said he wanted to warn people there to get ready—that there probably would be some bad publicity hitting the newspapers before long.

11

True Love

John Daly had been disingenuous when he put such a fine point on not having had any sponsors during his first year on the PGA Tour. Actually, he had a number of pay-for-performance contracts with the manufacturers of equipment he used. Each of these agreements would yield up to $50,000 should he win a tournament. What the deals didn't provide were large retainer fees. Daly would be compensated for achievement with his sponsors' products, not for being John Daly.

As the people at Wilson Sporting Goods, who weren't affiliated with Daly, monitored the unabated love-fest that began between him and his fans during the second round at Crooked Stick, they recognized this man was a bonanza of a golf-equipment endorsement program waiting to happen. Daly played exceptional golf at the PGA Championship, but it didn't slip by the people at Wilson that a goodly portion of his appeal was fan identification. Since many people who watch golf also play it, the notion that thousands of the faithful would cue up to buy John Daly golf equipment was almost self-evident.

Golf equipment is normally marketed by performance characteristics—the most forgiving club or the most water-resistant shoe. This is especially true for golf balls, and there are as many brands and styles of balls in pro shops as there are beverages at 7-Eleven. The balls vary by construction, cover materials, dimple patterns, and other, even more esoteric, considerations—all of which tend to confound weekend golfers who don't read two or three golf magazines a month. Imagine the simplicity, then, of being able to walk in and request a sleeve of those John Daly balls. Besides, they had to travel exceptionally far, right?

The folks at Wilson Sporting Goods called in Daly's managers and began filling wheelbarrows with money in front of them. They said to give a holler when the piles got high enough. Daly's people nodded for them to keep stacking, while reminding everyone that even though he had won only one tournament, John's future was unlimited. They had said that right there on TV. The agents ultimately felt some compassion and let the company off for a reported $4 million, payable over the four years of the agreement.

Combined with his other endorsements and deals and his ten-year PGA Tour exemption, the Wilson pact allowed Daly to go into the 1992 season with no dire financial pressure to win a golf tournament or even to finish well in a few of them. He had become the first celebrity golfer: someone who, without a track record on the tour, was being paid extremely well for being famous, likable, and entertaining. Although he might want to win every tournament he entered for his own satisfaction, one of his most important responsibilities to his sponsors was to remain popular with the galleries.

Daly knew his sweetheart deal with Wilson wasn't going to improve his standing with his fellow members of the PGA Tour, most of whom wouldn't earn in five years what Daly had already corralled in one. With very few exceptions, they would never garner the fan support Daly had. The temptation would be understandably strong to hiss "And he's only won one damn tournament" after learning of the latest Daly windfall.

Daly's unprecedented rise to prominence was also causing him to come under increased scrutiny by the tour administration. Having some kid from Arkansas who was playing the Hogan Tour hospitalized with alcohol poisoning would produce normal concern for the boy's health among the administration. Having the same thing happen to a PGA champion with this kind of visibility would be like the Republicans having it happen to their presidential candidate. People would get apoplectic.

Trying to prevent this, tour employees had been talking to Daly about giving up the beer. He told them to hit the pike, as his alcohol problems were behind him. He allowed as things had sometimes gotten out of control when he was still communing with Jack Daniel's, but he had beaten the bottle, and—don't ever forget this—he had done it on his own. So don't talk to John Daly about a beer problem. There was no beer problem. As Daly was fond of saying, you can't take everything away from a person's past. Most emphatically, they were not depriving him of his beer.

All of the bad or annoying things that had happened to Daly lately seemed to have a similar origin—they began when other people got into his face uninvited. The people who called about Bettye didn't know John Daly, but they sashayed into his business like they were kin. The other players on the tour were talking trash, when anybody could see they were jealous. Then the tour office started with the beer—never mind that their information could only be coming from the players, who were like brown-nosing kids running to the teacher behind his back. No way was Daly going to let this stuff get to him.

It was with this new air of resolve that Daly arrived in

Carlsbad, California, for the Tournament of Champions during the second week of January 1992 with his brother, Jamie—his faithful and dedicated drinking buddy of long standing—along as a traveling companion. John wasn't going to let the flu he had picked up bother him, nor the 75 he shot during the first round. He was determined to focus on the positive stuff, such as the 1991 Rookie of the Year Award he received at the PGA Tour's annual banquet Thursday evening. It felt terrific to have his peers clapping for him the way they did when his name was called.

ABC was broadcasting the tournament, and their announcer, Brent Musburger, asked Daly if they could tape an interview. He said sure, because you never refused face time before a national audience, and how bad could a TV interview be, anyway? The networks' sports programming divisions had a quasi-financial relationship with the PGA Tour that seemed to subliminally discourage most of their interviewers from asking hardball questions. Naturally, the broadcast of golf tournaments was underwritten by commercials, but often the PGA Tour fostered or coordinated the sale of that time for the networks. The normal way for a corporation to become the title sponsor of a tournament was to put up prize money and buy a mandated block of time for TV commercials. Without this arrangement, most tournaments wouldn't be seen on TV because the ratings were too low.

Daly sat down in front of the cameras not suspecting anything was amiss. Then Musburger blindsided him by asking about his drinking beer during the PGA Championship, destroying a hotel room in Jamaica, and purposely signing an incorrect scorecard in that country. Where the hell did this come from? Nobody in the press had touched the beer story, and what did anything that happened overseas have to do with playing golf in California?

Daly denied the beer and the scorecard stories, and admitted to one incident of violence to a hotel room—although he didn't correct Musburger's having incorrectly located the hotel in Jamaica rather than South Africa—before lashing out at his fellow pros, whom he saw as being behind this. "A lot of players are starting some stuff," he said, "and I think they ought to come to me and say it. But they're too scared to do that. If somebody has got something to say, say it to my face. I might hit them. I might not."

Regardless of how he felt, Daly committed a major breach of tour etiquette in going public with his feud with the players. Tour business was supposed to be taken care of in-house and behind soundproof doors. Whatever problems he had before with the players would become much more intractable. If that weren't bad enough, Daly went on in the interview to forsake what was left of his privacy by volunteering that Bettye and he were "no longer together right now" because "some serious things came down in Jamaica."

The interview aired on Sunday, as Daly was on his way to finishing tied for twenty-first place, and he was able to slip out of town before anyone from the media could make a bigger story out of his open challenge to the rest of the PGA Tour or his announcement about Bettye.

Daly had to travel only a hundred miles from his location on the Pacific coast of California to reach the next tournament site near Palm Springs, in the southern California desert. It was a five-round pro-am event called the Bob Hope Chrysler Classic. With the veteran entertainer as the tournament's host, there was sure to be a squad of pretty young girls lolling about for embellishment. While this was a golf tournament that was being staged, and not a Christmas or entertaining-the-troops TV special, having girls in sexy cheerleader outfits as a backdrop was Hope's idea of how you showed people a good time. It was meant to suggest the glamour and sophistication of old Hollywood.

John Daly's exceptional flexibility was evident by the time he was fifteen.

RAY HENTGES

The 1983 Missouri Class 1A-3A High School champion golf team: (from left) Scott Cassmeyer, Chris Hentges, coach Ray Hentges, John Daly, and Brad Struttman.

RAY HENTGES

As a high school senior, Daly's nickname was the Pillsbury Dough Boy.

BROTHER JAMES ABELL

Newly slim, Daly was voted Arkansas Golfer
of the Year in 1986.

THE ARKANSAS DEMOCRAT-GAZETTE

Rick Ross was Daly's friend and golf teacher when he returned to Dardanelle.

WILLIAM WARTMAN

Petey King, Daly's roomate, teammate, and drinking companion at the University of Arkansas.

WILLIAM WARTMAN

University of Arkansas golf coach Bill Woodley tried unsuccessfully to get Daly to stop drinking.

WILLIAM WARTMAN

Daly thanks Kevin Ryals for writing a song about him for John Daly Day in Dardanelle, Arkansas.

THE ARKANSAS DEMOCRAT-GAZETTE

(from left) John's mother, Lou, his Uncle Ben, and Aunt Ann watch him win the 1991 PGA Championship on TV.

THE ARKANSAS DEMOCRAT-GAZETTE

Daly's family now runs the Highway 22 Convenience Store and John Daly Golf Shop in Dardanelle.

WILLIAM WARTMAN

Bettye Fulford congratulates her boyfriend on winning the 1991 PGA Championship.

JOHN GENTRY

Curtis Strange (right background) would have harsh words for Daly after he accused fellow pro golfers of using cocaine.

Paulette Dean (in "Classic" sweater) would become John Daly's third wife after they met at Bob Hope's golf tournament.

STEVEN SCHRETZMANN, *THE DESERT SUN*

With his cap concealing his shaved head, Daly slaps high-five with his caddie after winning the BellSouth Classic.

KEVIN KEISTER, *ATLANTA JOURNAL-CONSTITUTION*

Given his immense popularity, Daly is sometimes escorted by more police officers than a presidential candidate.

KEVIN KEISTER, *ATLANTA JOURNAL-CONSTITUTION*

All of this worked for John Daly, and while he was playing in a pretournament event, the Hope Chrysler Classic girls—each had one of the three words of the event title on her sweater—caught his eye. There was one in particular he liked. She was a pretty blonde with nicely tanned legs, a huge smile, and a thick mop of hair, and she displayed the word *Classic* across her chest. Her name was Paulette Dean, and she was a twenty-year-old model from Palm Desert who was there because she was working. She knew nothing about golf and had never heard of John Daly. With what was shaking out with Bettye at the moment, nothing sounded better to Daly than anonymity. He invited Paulette to dinner, and when she accepted, he asked if she might not be able to find a girlfriend for his brother, Jamie.

Dinner was so enjoyable that John and Paulette began hitting the bars in the Palm Springs area every night, sometimes in the company of the women who were *Hope* and *Chrysler* in their work clothes. John was drinking heavily, and was instantly recognizable, so he became the center of attention as they cruised the hot spots. Paulette wasn't a big drinker and didn't like noisy bars that much, but she went along and didn't seem to mind that John drank, smoked, and raised hell to excess. One evening Daly's group was asked to leave Cost's, the nightclub in the local Marriott hotel, because they were causing such a commotion.

Normally John would have been in love by this point, but the situation with Bettye wasn't resolved—and Marvin Mitchelson wasn't pleased about that. After several weeks of warning Daly's people that they'd better get a settlement offer—one involving money and a house—on the table, Mitchelson had gotten nowhere. He decided to tighten the screws a bit and allow Daly to have a preview of what his life was going to be like when Mitchelson jumped on his back wearing cleats.

On the first day of the Bob Hope tournament, Mitchelson issued a press release announcing that he had been retained by Bettye Fulford, but he didn't say any more. This didn't provoke a response from Daly, and the next day Mitchelson informed the Associated Press that Bettye was pregnant, and that if a settlement wasn't reached in the next week, he was going to file palimony and paternity actions with the courts.

As Mitchelson could have predicted, the sportswriters leaped into pursuit of Daly, trying to get his comments on the situation for their newspapers. This was the first public airing of the story, but Daly didn't shrink from the reporters in fear, mumbling "no comment." That would have been the correct strategy for someone interested in protecting his image. But this wasn't about something as simplistic as public relations to Daly. It was about right and wrong. His heart had been broken by a deceitful woman, and he was certain that if the public knew what Bettye had done, they would agree that she didn't deserve a cent. When the reporters called or tracked him down at the tournament, Daly was only too happy to recount Bettye's lies.

"It's hard to believe someone could be that crooked, that mean," he said. "It makes me look stupid. Here I go with this girl for a year and a half and I don't know how old she is or that she had a kid. She just lies. All she did is lie to me the whole time. If you gave her a lie test, she wouldn't pass one of them. She has crushed my whole life. I will never trust a woman again. I still love her. I'll always love her. I feel like I have to start my life over."

Meanwhile, Bettye's divorce from Michael Blackshear had come through on January 6, and she had started calling John at the tournament in Carlsbad, saying that she wanted to see him. John said that he might want to sit down and talk to her, but he wasn't sure if he was ready for it yet. All he needed was for her to start lying again and he would go nuts. Still, he wanted to hear her explain why she had gone running to Marvin Mitchelson the instant he broke up with her. So when Bettye called the following week and said she wanted to come to Palm Desert and see John, he—amid the salvos both sides were firing in the press—told her to come on ahead. Just to keep things amusing, Daly played in a foursome at the tournament on Saturday that included the Vice President of the United States, Dan "Family Values" Quayle. Appropriately, Daly missed the cut.

As the Daly boys were traveling to the next tournament, in Phoenix, Arizona, Bettye had her lawyers issue a statement to the press saying that she was very upset that John was publicly questioning whether the baby was his. There was no doubt, she had them say, whose child this was. Her lawyers also issued another ultimatum: Respond to the financial demands they had made in a settlement offer, or they were going to court.

John continued to celebrate his status as a newly unattached man in Phoenix—although Paulette Dean was in the process of becoming his new girlfriend. The Phoenix tournament attracts the largest galleries in the world—over 400,000 for the week—and Daly partied every night with the multitudes in an open-air bar that was set up in a tent at the tournament site under the clear Arizona sky. This was better than it had ever been at the University of Arkansas. Daly was acutely famous now, and the people in the tent couldn't believe he was right there drinking with them. Professional golfers virtually never socialize with the hoi polloi on the tournament grounds, and the fans loved Daly for sharing the communion of the hops with them.

Daly's golf game wasn't on that week, as he finished tied for sixty-third place in the tournament. Developments on the domestic front weren't any better. Bettye's lawyers were about to file a $1 million palimony suit and a separate paternity suit.

John's life was as tempestuous as ever, yet there was one decided difference. Every week now there was a sparkling bit of good news waiting under his pillow for Daly when he woke up. This week it was his being named professional athlete of the year by the Tennessee Sports Hall of Fame in a ceremony at the Holiday Inn in Nashville. Plus things were sure to quiet down on the domestic front when Daly went off on an appearance-fee-plus-expenses trip to Australia.

Appearance fees were offered to the top golfers as an inducement to play in tournaments everywhere in the world except the United States, where they were banned in PGA Tour events. When golfers win additional money from the purses of events they're paid to play in, it makes for profitable travel. Daly looked like he was going to clean up on his Australian trip when he earned $69,000 in a Skins Game at Port Douglas, on his first of two stops.

In Melbourne the following week the pace of play at the Australian Masters was especially slow—almost five and a half hours for eighteen holes—and Daly found himself getting annoyed. He shot a four over for the round, then lost a ball in a tree the next day on the fourteenth hole, and that did it. Two holes later, he decided he was out of there. Right on the course, he instructed his manager to book seats on the next flight home. He finished the day with an 81, giving him a two-day score that was well above the projected cut. Daly could have signed his scorecard, collected his $35,000 appearance fee, and left. Instead, he refused to sign the scorecard, which disqualified him from the tournament but didn't affect his appearance fee.

It was strange behavior, but it wasn't only John who was acting curiously at this time. Back in Tennessee, Bettye had unilaterally withdrawn both of her suits against John without providing an explanation—or receiving a penny of settlement money.

On the long flight home, John had time to stew about the crap he was getting of late, and he decided he knew how to fix it. Before his next tournament, in La Jolla, California, John took his checkbook, visited a recreational-vehicle dealer in San Diego, and bought $150,000 worth of the god-damn-dest motor home they had on the lot. Forty-feet long, with two telephones, two televisions, a satellite dish, a washer and dryer, kitchen, bathroom—the works. John then tossed the keys to Jamie, found a place for Paulette's stuff, and hit the open road. No more staying in hotels, with people watching his every move, or flying in airplanes, where he'd get nervous. John Daly would be mobile. He'd roll into a campground, hook up some hoses and lines, and he'd be home. He could howl at the moon naked out there if he wanted to, and no one would give a damn.

Spring

John Daly had been devastated in December 1991 when he came to accept that Bettye Fulford had lied to him. He was blown away a second time only a few weeks later when, of all things, reporters galore wrote about the personal lives of Bettye and him after he freely gave this information to one after another of them. Daly's press coverage had been so adoring—and so forgiving—for so long that it was as though he'd come to believe reporters were his press agents.

The stuff that was written and said about him irked him enough that he was itching for the chance to tell someone how he felt about it. That opportunity surfaced in March when commentator Gary McCord, who had nearly canonized Daly at the PGA Championship, interviewed him during the early rounds of another tournament. McCord asked Daly a question about his image, and Daly replied on live TV that he "couldn't give a shit" what the public thought about him.

The truth of the situation was that this remark was aired during a golf tournament on a cable network on a weekday. The viewing audience probably didn't exceed the population

126

of Dardanelle, and most of those watching likely used the profane word at least once during every round of golf they played. The reality of the situation, though, was that this was the PGA Tour, where the mascot wasn't an oversized animal or a cartoon character. It was a choirboy. Everyone warned Daly there would be repercussions.

When he showed up for the Players Championship in Ponte Vedra, Florida, at the end of March 1992, Daly had a stress-related rash, and he wouldn't have been at all surprised if it had been caused by his dealings with the media. That was why, when he shot a 68 during Thursday's round and was asked to come to the pressroom, he refused. That prompted an offer that couldn't be declined—a directive to report to the office of PGA Tour commissioner Deane Beman, which, since this event was held at the tour's headquarters, was just across the way.

Beman, fifty-three, was in his nineteenth year as the head of the tour, a time during which he had brought unimagined prosperity to professional golf while managing to personally alienate an amazingly high percentage of the people he dealt with. He was a short, plump, combative man who liked to flash his commissioner's badge wherever he got the chance. In another era, he would have worn cleats on his wingtips to announce his presence. For a defiant, fractious, but sometimes insecure man like John Daly, Deane Beman was the closest thing there was to a natural predator.

During their meeting, Beman cautioned Daly about using profanity, saying he had received five or six letters of complaint from viewers who had heard what Daly said. Beman also told Daly he would be fined if he refused to go to the media room again in the future. Although Beman technically worked for the players, since the PGA Tour was their association, he was nearly omnipotent in his ability to penalize or discipline them, and he was seldom challenged. Daly left Beman's office convinced of only one thing—that this old dude needed to get off his back.

Daly's visit with Beman did nothing to improve Daly's attitude, and that was the kiss of death for his golf game. It essentially guaranteed that he was going to play badly. Daly was entirely a feel player—as opposed to a mechanics guy—and when such a golfer is upset, his tactile senses are short-circuited. He might as well go home.

That was exactly what Daly was trying to do when, hopelessly out of contention, he and Mark Calcavecchia—a player slightly older than Daly, but of a similarly excitable temperament—decided to see how quickly they could play their final round at the Players Championship on Sunday. They were the first twosome off in the morning, when the grass was still rich with dew, and they raced through their rounds of 80 and 81 in a bit over two hours. On some holes they tried to hit their tee balls simultaneously. They believed they were providing entertainment for the few fans who were around that early in the day, while having some fun for themselves. When he heard about their antics, Deane Beman decreed that Daly and Calcavecchia had engaged in conduct unbecoming to professional golfers, and he sent word through his minions that they would be fined.

Daly and Calcavecchia's greatest misdeed may have been that they weren't Greg Norman and Mark O'Meara. During the season-ending Nabisco Championship in 1988, Norman and O'Meara found themselves out of contention—and out of the limelight—in an important tournament. Unlike Daly and Calcavecchia, however, Norman and O'Meara hadn't just quietly decided between themselves to have some fun. They publicly announced before their round that they were going to set a record for the fastest round ever played on the PGA Tour—although no such official figure existed, for obvious reasons.

Then they, their caddies, and the volunteer scorers set off jogging from shot to shot over the rambling seaside course at Pebble Beach, California, while their gallery shouted encouragement and called out their elapsed time after each shot. Norman and O'Meara eventually finished their eighteen holes in one hour and twenty-four minutes, with both players scoring a 79. Rather than being fined for playing a round in more than thirty minutes less than Daly and Calcavecchia would take, Norman and O'Meara were celebrated, as scoreboards around the course flashed the twosome's time and spectators applauded them for their efforts to entertain them.

Deane Beman might have been upset at Norman and O'Meara—although he never gave any public indication he was—but he wouldn't have dreamed of challenging them. They—and especially Norman—were wealthy journeyman golfers who wouldn't be cowed by Beman for a second. It was a mind-set after John Daly's own heart.

Daly took the week after the Players Championship off to prepare for his first Masters Tournament, while people in Georgia were also getting ready for his arrival. The practice range at Augusta National Golf Club was only 260 yards long, and it terminated at Washington Road, which was always choked with traffic during tournament week. The club had erected a fifty-foot screen there in front of a stand of trees to keep range balls from clobbering passers-by, but club officials had predicted—correctly—that Daly would be able to clear the screen easily. They raised it by 15 feet in his honor.

The first thing Daly did when he got to the range was yank out his driver and shoot for the fence. He got one or two over, and the spectators went nuts. The Masters Tournament prides itself on its knowledgeable fans, who applaud only when it is appropriate, but people went berserk at haughty Augusta National, just as they did everywhere else, when Daly had a driver in his hands and he was whipping it for all he was worth. Then again, this was a day for practice rounds, when anyone could walk in off the street and buy a pass. Tickets for the tournament itself were spoken for years in advance, but one couldn't be quite certain of the pedigrees of those attending practice days.

Whoever they were, two to three times as many of them flocked around Daly as anyone else—including Jack Nicklaus, who, with his six Masters titles, was royalty there. Daly played a practice round on Wednesday with his good buddy Fuzzy Zoeller, and the two of them clicked with each other and their fans. Daly and Zoeller were feeling relaxed and comfortable, smoking cigarettes, making jokes, and signing autographs for the crowd. That's why it didn't seem so unusual when a man pushed forward from the swarm with some papers in his hands as Daly walked from the ninth green to the tenth tee. He asked Daly if he was John Daly, which was such a joke, then he handed Daly the papers and hurried away. In the middle of a practice round for his first Masters Tournament—one of the most prestigious events in golf—Bettye Fulford's lawyers had just had John Daly served with papers for a new palimony and paternity suit.

Bettye had withdrawn the suit in Tennessee, where there was no precedent for palimony cases, and established a residence for herself in her old home state of Georgia. Her lawyers then waited for the Masters Tournament to roll around, knowing that Daly would be there and that a process server could gain access to the golf club during the practice rounds. Daly handed the papers to his caddie without looking at them, and it was good that he didn't, for reading that his career had improved in large part due to Bettye's encouragement and motivation wouldn't have done him any good. Nor would knowing that this suit, in addition to palimony and child support, also asked for punitive damages "in amount sufficient to deter the defendant from similar conduct."

It could have been such a humiliating thing, having this happen in front of his fans, but when reporters asked him, Daly insisted it wasn't. "This is the Masters, man," he said. "Nothing is going to hurt me this week. Nothing."

Daly was strictly kicking back and keeping it low-key and low-stress to insure there was no interference with his game.

Wednesday night he visited Augusta's finest nudie bar and had a few brews. Then, later in the week, he got lonely and began thinking that since they were both in the same state, what the hell—and he invited Bettye over.

Things hadn't been going that well with Paulette Dean, and she and Daly were taking a break. As time went on, John realized he missed Bettye a lot. He was thinking about her at night plenty of times. They had been all over the place and done everything together. She was going to have his baby, and when he was alone and could block the lawyer stuff out of his mind, he realized that he had never loved anybody as much as he loved that woman. He didn't want to relinquish that.

Bettye and John talked things over. She said she had lied to him only because she loved him so much. She was afraid she would lose him if he knew the truth about her history and her age. They both agreed that everything had been blown out of proportion by the lawyers—you could see it in the way the lawyers were always saying it was the people around John and Bettye who were doing the manipulating, not the lawyers.

John finished tied for nineteenth in his first Masters, which was decent—but he didn't really care. He had a junket coming up in a few weeks to play in the Italian Open, and he and Bettye were going to go over early. They were headed for scenic Venice, where John was going to have the most wonderful and romantic vacation of his life. It would be Venice in the spring, with the gondolas gliding through the shimmering water and the light playing off the stones in the magnificent courtyards. They were leaving on this capricious getaway as soon as possible—right after Bettye withdrew all her outstanding legal actions against John.

After Venice, they arrived in Monticello, Italy, on April 30 for the tournament. With Bettye now eight months pregnant, John felt compelled to announce the good news to the press. He and Bettye were to be united in holy matrimony. "We haven't set a date for the marriage, but we want to marry," he said. "We would love to marry, but I have been on the road for several weeks and I have a busy schedule throughout May."

Asked about their raging battles of recent months, John said that it had all grown out of miscommunications between their lawyers.

The happy couple retired to their hotel, and on Sunday, who should John run into in the lobby but Sylvester Stallone! And—get out—he recognized John. Turned out Stallone was a golf nut, and he wanted to have a beer with John right there in the damn hotel lobby in Monticello, Italy. John and Rambo hanging out—or was it Rocky Daly and Sylvester Stallone? Whatever, the important thing was nothing got busted up or anything. If that wasn't something. How many times did Sylvester Stallone recognize someone who wasn't a movie star? It couldn't be much.

John called and told his parents to get the house in Dardanelle ready for a wedding. The Episcopal minister came over, along with a couple of dozen guests. Bettye didn't have any family there. No one had ever heard her talk about anyone other than one aunt, and the common understanding was that she had been orphaned as a child. John and Bettye were married on May 8. After Italy, they didn't really need a honeymoon, but John had planned a canoe and Jeep trip in the backwoods of Arkansas with Jamie at this time, and they went ahead with that.

With the baby's arrival imminent, John had taken out a permit to increase the size of their 2,600-square-foot house near Memphis by 50 percent, but Bettye reasserted her previous position that living in the vicinity of his drinking buddies wasn't a good place for her new husband-to-be. John allowed that if they were going to move, Castle Rock, Colorado, where he had played in the International, might be the perfect place. It was remote, peaceful, and quiet there, and if he and Bettye were going to start all over, those could be the magical elements they needed to make it work.

Despite his busy schedule, Daly attended a media day at Bellerive Country Club in St. Louis on May 11. The club was going to be the site of the 1992 PGA Championship and, as defending champion, he felt an obligation to appear. While he was at the course and the media were close at hand, John said that there was something he had to tell the assembled media representatives. Then he announced that he and Bettye had gotten married the previous Friday and that they were "going to make it work the best way they could.

"We've got a baby girl coming," he said. "We're very happy. I hope we can live the rest of our lives together."

The reporters asked Daly how it felt to be married again, and he remarked that he was glad he'd be able to concentrate on his golf more, now that his domestic situation was under control. But he told the media folks that he did have one concern about his new status as a father-to-be.

Bettye's pregnancy was an overriding factor in John's decision to forget Bettye's past deceptions and marry her. That had often gotten lost amid all their fighting and press releases. Now, with the child's birth at hand, John began thinking about the ways in which his life was going to change. Inevitably, he recalled his own childhood, and there were aspects of that which frightened him.

"I'm scared to death about being a father. I don't know much about being one," he said, remembering how things could be unpleasant at home. "I know my dad wanted to hit me about a hundred thousand times."

Thunder in the Pines

With his wedding out of the way and his relationship with Bettye now legally defined, it was time for John Daly to get back to earning a living, which in this case meant playing a couple of tournaments in Texas. John and Bettye, Jamie and his girlfriend, and John's caddie and his girlfriend all piled into the motor home and embarked across the wide-open highways that led to the Lone Star State. John recorded a tie for twenty-ninth and a missed cut, and then they turned the house on wheels around and charted a path east to the Maryland suburbs of the District of Columbia.

It was the end of May, and Bettye was due to give birth momentarily. Bettye told John that if he was on the course when she went into labor, he should finish his round before coming to the hospital. Afterward, when reporters asked John what he intended to do in that situation, he said offhandedly, "It depends on how I'm playing."

Despite being heavy with child, Bettye trailed John around all eighteen holes of the sloping and sometimes precipitous course in Potomac on Friday. John was in contention, and it was like old times. Bettye and he were in love and on the road, and his game had suddenly dropped into the groove. The spectators were cheering so thunderously for him that the roar intruded on golfers playing five holes ahead. These moments were what defined golf for John Daly.

With a chance to win the tournament on Sunday, he fed off the crowd, as he had at Crooked Stick. Some of the other players—and particularly the older ones—might complain he was showboating, and the sportswriters might keep referring to his horrendous driving-accuracy statistics. But Daly didn't play for either of these groups. He played for his fans. He never wanted their admiration to end, and they showed no signs of pulling back. Even when, as on this day, needing a birdie on the eighteenth to win, Daly shot bogey and finished tied for second place.

Bettye and John's daughter, Shynah—a name that came to John while he was listening to Bad Company sing "Shooting Star"—was born on June 10 in Memphis, while John was in the midst of missing three consecutive cuts. That may have made John a little frisky when he returned to Castle Rock, Colorado, on June 22 to play in a charity exhibition called Thunder in the Pines. The event matched Daly with another long-hitting pro, Davis Love III, in an explosive display of high-altitude golf.

At the inevitable press conference that accompanied these competitions, John joked that he would have either an Egg McMuffin or a Miller Lite for breakfast before playing in a tournament. Then, after a tiring day at the course, and facing a red-eye flight to the East Coast to play in yet another tournament, John and his caddie, Greg Rita, stopped before boarding the plane and actually had a few beers.

Things started going awry the minute Daly and Rita boarded the 12:50 A.M. Continental flight from Stapleton Airport to Newark. There weren't two contiguous seats available in the first-class cabin, and when Rita asked for help with his carry-on luggage, the female flight attendant declined, citing a bad back. When the same woman went to close the cabin door, Daly made some caustic remarks about her troublesome back.

Daly and Rita were soon off the plane, with Continental Airlines believing that its flight crew asked the two men to leave and the men believing they did it voluntarily. The entire incident might have ended there, but when Daly subsequently withdrew from the tournament he was flying to, the Buick Open in Westchester County, New York, some officials there became miffed, because regardless of how he played, John Daly sold tickets.

Someone from the tournament made a statement to reporters on Tuesday, saying that Daly had been thrown off the plane because he was drunk. Stories were written relaying this information. When they got back to Daly, he got furious and began insisting that: A. he hadn't been drunk; B. it was the airline crew that was at fault, not him; C. he had left the plane voluntarily; and D. it was so unfair that everyone was always picking on him about his drinking—especially when he wasn't even drunk!

Despite the misfortunes Daly had had in his personal life when he was playing at Castle Pines Golf Club—Bettye's shoulder being injured, then the incident on the plane—the Dalys went ahead and purchased a house there that summer. It was a $565,000, 6,500-square-foot affair, with five bedrooms spread over three stories. It was in a gated community, up in the woods, and the house overlooked the fifteenth hole of the Castle Pines golf course.

With a healthy baby and a stunning home in the mountains added to his life, it should have been a happy time for John Daly, but it wasn't. Except for the Maryland tournament, he was in a slump. He wasn't playing golf worth a damn that summer, and he needed to win another tournament so people would stop whispering behind his back that he was a one-shot wonder and so some of the guys on the tour wouldn't be able to call him "Long Gone Daly" anymore. But it didn't happen, and he would get incredibly angry and depressed—such as the time that year when he and Bettye and the baby were in the car, and while approaching a red light, with cross traffic moving through the intersection, he refused to stop or slow down. All Bettye could do was scream and thank God that they squeezed through without being killed.

Daly came to St. Louis in August to defend his PGA title, and he was in a philosophical mood at his pretournament press conference. He said that the previous year he had been "the underdog of all underdogs. It was a dream that came true so fast that I couldn't think about it being a dream until after it was over. It was the best four days of my life. There was skill, luck, maybe even destiny."

Daly wasn't at all pleased with what was being written about him, and he wasn't afraid to say it. "Some reporters or newspapers haven't written the facts about some of the things I've said. Some of the things I've said in a positive way have been turned around and make me look bad. A lot written about John Daly hasn't been fair, which is life.

"I just want to get on with my life, and they don't need to be writing about me unless I'm on the leaderboard. I'm just sorry that it had to come down to this. But until they stop treating my life like a soap opera, I'm not going to talk to them."

To blow off steam, Daly went to the practice range. With reporters—as well as spectators—within earshot, he prepared to smash one of his trademark drives. "This," he said before swinging the club violently at the ball, "is for all the media that has written bad articles about me."

Warming to his task, Daly continued his offensive when Jim Nantz of CBS asked to tape an interview during the tournament. Daly pounced on the opportunity, using the airtime to castigate his inquisitor from ABC, Brent Musburger, as the worst announcer he had ever seen in golf; he attacked Buick—which was the title sponsor of four (four!) PGA Tour events—because someone at a tournament they sponsored said Daly had been drunk. He said he would never buy one of the cars made by the biggest automotive sponsor on the tour.

The tour's headquarters in Florida was a thousand miles away from St. Louis, but even as Daly's interview was being aired on Saturday afternoon, reporters could hear a computer printer cranking out the paperwork for the substantial fine that was going to be levied against Daly. No one broached the topic with him until the next day, when he was asked if he anticipated that Deane Beman would penalize him.

"If he wants to fine me for something like that, for speaking the truth, I feel really sorry for him," Daly said. "I feel like the players should be able to speak up for themselves. It's about time that a player tells the media and people like that to get their facts straight."

One year after Daly had been termed the most exciting thing to happen to golf in decades, a good bit of the brightness had disappeared from his story. The sports editor of his hometown newspaper in Memphis took him to task, saying whoever was advising Daily was doing a poor job and that Daly had to learn how to manage the media, not run away from it. Steve Hershey, the golf writer for *USA Today*, was even more dismissive, saying people had seen Daly as a breath of fresh air but that he was turning out to be "an ill wind, blowing in tales of destruction, drunkenness, and deceit."

Through it all, there were two constants: John Daly's behavior and his bond with his fans. Nowhere did these two factors meld more harmoniously than the following month at the B.C. Open in Endicott, New York. It was late September, where they stick tournaments that don't have corporate sponsors, and therefore won't have television coverage. Rather than being named for a business entity, this tournament was titled after a comic strip—B.C.—whose creator was a native son. His Stone Age title character was depicted everywhere at the event, and the strip's creator brought in his famous cartoonist friends for the preliminary festivities. While other tournaments entertained the visiting pros lavishly and treated caddies like carriers of communicable diseases, at the B.C. they held a caddie golf tournament.

The tournament course wasn't a deluxe resort layout but a public club called the En-Joie, from when it was the domain of the ten thousand employees of Endicott-Johnson shoe company, and because people wanted visitors to have a good time at the club. Endicott was a nineteenth-century factory town in the approach to the Adirondacks. Most of the plants in the area had closed, but the people stayed and found ways to eke out a living because, after all, their families were there. Life didn't stop just because the Industrial Revolution was over. Manhattan was a couple of hundred miles to the southeast, but you could rent a house here for what a space in a parking garage cost there.

You could see a history of ancestors arriving at Ellis Island in every face in town. There were Italians and Poles and Greeks and Eastern Europeans—people of short stature with sharp features and some pigment to their skin. The men wore windbreakers with a logo from their union, VFW post, or their church. The women weren't bashful about coloring their hair if they wanted—red or brunette or blond—but none of this complicated highlighting business. When people did something here, they did it directly. If John Daly had been a goddamn Yankee, as they say in Arkansas, he could have been raised in Endicott.

That was why, when he and Bettye and Shynah were out for the evening on the Wednesday night before the tournament started, everyone pretended not to notice while he was consuming nearly three six-packs of beer as though it were water and he was a man in great thirst. They nodded when he walked out after midnight as erectly as he had walked in, as they did the next morning when he appeared at the first tee before nine. On a day when most men would have encamped under the covers, waiting for their stupefying hangover to relent, John Daly shot a 67, putting him two shots off the lead in a competition against some of the finest golfers in the world.

It wasn't a pretty round, as he hit only four greens in regulation, but his short game was there. On Friday he shot a 66, on a narrow course with tight fairways and lots of trees—precisely the type of layout he wasn't supposed to be able to play. Then on Saturday, when the big crowds came out, so did the rain. This was so fortuitous for Daly that it could be argued that it was a sign of approval from God. Daly shot his second bogey-free round, a 67, and never lost his composure throughout an extended delay during the downpour.

"We waited on every shot. It was a very, very slow day. I felt like I held my patience real well. Usually if it takes that long to play golf . . . ," Daly said in his press conference, and then stopped. He decided he wasn't going to remind everyone of what he did when he lost his temper. "We were out there for six, seven hours today. I was really proud of myself for holding my patience."

The townspeople filed into the En-Joie Golf Club after church and bacon and eggs on Sunday, carrying their umbrellas to ward off the light rain. Daly came out and carded a 66. He was one shot off the tournament record and six ahead of his closest competitor. It was Crooked Stick revisited. All of the spectators on the grounds, except for the claustrophobic, were trotting after him, whooping and screaming like it was a rodeo.

Coming up the eighteenth fairway, with chills running through his body, his heart pounding, and the hair standing up on his arms, Daly felt intense excitement overlain with relief. He didn't care what anybody said; he didn't think the first tournament was the hardest one to win. He thought it was the second. Now he had broken through that curse.

They often give the leader of a golf tournament an armed police escort during his final round on Sunday, although the B.C. Open seemed to be the last place on earth where someone might try to harm John Daly. During the awards ceremony on the eighteenth green, where they presented Daly with his trophy and $144,000 check, he acknowledged the troopers who had accompanied him. "I've got to thank everybody that came out—especially the police officers," he said, while addressing the crowd. "It's nice to be close to them, knowing they're not going to put handcuffs on you."

The sportswriters were quick to praise Daly for his decisive win at the B.C., and that seemed to placate him. He kept a low profile through most of the fall, but when he appeared at an exhibition match in California in the middle of November, he was asked about his relations with the media. "I've had some good and bad press, but bad press is better than no press at all," he said.

Merely five weeks would pass before John Daly would rethink that remark. In that time, he pretty much stopped playing golf. It was the minuscule off-season for the tour, Daly wasn't in any TV events, and he certainly wasn't going to play golf at home. He was living a mile up into the foothills of the Rocky Mountains, and it was December. Daly was doing a lot of hanging around the house with time on his hands, and that wasn't something Bettye Daly approved of. She always said that was when the trouble began—like the Sunday School adage said: Idle hands are the Devil's workshop.

With the Dalys living far removed from John's drinking buddies, the boys down South talked a lot about how Bettye had assumed total control of John's off-the-golf-course life.

Sometimes when the buddies spoke with John on the phone, he would say as much. He would complain that Bettye was mothering him to death—trying to dictate his time, dictate his friends, dictate what he did, what parties they went to, when they went home. She could be like the fascist of his life, and he was getting tired of it.

The Dalys had people in for a pre-Christmas weekend soiree in Castle Rock on December 19. Among others, Jamie Daly was there with a date, as was Dan Hampton, a hulking former Chicago Bears defensive lineman who was in town to be a sportscaster at the upcoming Denver Broncos football game. One of the many unexpected rewards that had come John's way as a result of his notoriety was the easy friendships it fostered with other professional athletes. Hampton was accompanied by a date, too, an attractive and outgoing young woman named Julie.

As the dark cold of the December evening descended outside the Daly house, Julie began showing a special interest in John while dodging the expected girl talk with Bettye. Bettye monitored this situation carefully and, as her blood alcohol level rose, she became annoyed, then jealous, before lashing out in anger in front of all their guests. She directed Hampton to exercise some jurisdiction over his girlfriend and reminded Julie, the young hussy, exactly who the mistress of the household was.

The rage that John Daly had been stockpiling since he had unloaded on a hotel room in South Africa the previous December suddenly detonated, as if spontaneous combustion were occurring in a grain silo. Some guests crouched against the blast and darted for the door; Hampton and his girlfriend evacuated to their room; and Bettye, after an exchange with John, scooped up Shynah and hid. The luxury home rocked with a cacophony of objects shattering from room to room and floor to floor.

When he was exhausted, Daly understood it was a cowardly thing that he had just done. He was ashamed and felt compelled to run. The door slammed and he scurried off into the night. His destination was the only place he could think to hide—Arkansas. It lay a thousand miles away across the plains in the dead of the winter night, the endless dormant fields interrupted only by the occasional midwestern town, its tidy houses aglow with Christmas lights.

Daly stopped periodically in the early morning to telephone his old friends and announce his impending arrival. He knew that he had hit the wall, that he had messed up big time, and that people were going to find out. He wanted to tell his friends his version of the night's events before they could get it from anyone else. He said that he was on the run, that he didn't know where he was going to go; his friends offered him places to stay.

Back in Colorado, Bettye Daly was receiving some late-arriving and uninvited guests: officers from the Douglas County sheriff's office. They had received an anonymous report that there had been trouble in the Dalys' home, and they were required by local law to come in and investigate. They found ponds of broken glass throughout the house from smashed pictures, broken windows, an overturned big-screen television, fractured liquor bottles, and splintered display cases. There were also jagged openings and blood splatters gracing the basement walls.

Although Bettye did not want to press charges against John, the police explained that the filing of third-degree assault charges was mandatory in domestic violence cases in Colorado. In the arrest affidavit the sheriff's office would prepare against John, the officers would report that Bettye had been thrown against the wall and her hair had been pulled, during the incident. The investigator contacted John's attorney and told him that if Daly did not return to

Colorado voluntarily to be arrested and charged, an arrest warrant would be issued for him. Daly drove back to Castle Rock to appear before a judge on Wednesday, December 21. He pleaded not guilty and posted $1,000 bond.

Daly's arraignment caused the affair to surface on the radar screens of reporters, and on Christmas the story began appearing in newspapers around the country. In addition to the basic information on the case, the *Rocky Mountain News* reported that "Bettye Daly had told investigators her husband's family had a history of alcoholism, and he had trouble controlling himself when he drank. Investigators said she had no visible marks or injuries and she said 'no bruises would show yet.'"

14

For Immediate Release

John Daly's holiday house-wrecking party wasn't the first time his drunkenness had put him and other people in danger. What was different about this episode was that if he was convicted as charged, he faced up to two years in prison. The situation was grave, yet Daly was a wealthy, prominent sports figure. Surely those around him realized this required immediate intervention by highly skilled and trained professionals. Ah, but they did. Shortly after Daly's arrest, the best talents his handlers could find were toiling over an exquisitely worded press release, working the spin for all it was worth.

A lawyer based in Washington, D.C.—as was Daly's management agency—produced a release quoting Bettye as saying, "I was not struck or physically injured in the incident. I neither reported the incident nor requested the sheriff's department to intervene." In John's section of the handout he was quoted as saying the incident was unfortunate, he deeply regretted it, and he and Bettye were "committed as a couple to working through this problem" in order to put it behind them. Bettye also asked that people respect their privacy.

Left to his own devices, Daly probably would have hidden out in his house at Castle Pines, staying out of the way of the repair crews, for a few weeks until people began to forget. Then he'd have gone back on the tour, smiling ruefully—but not talking—whenever anyone asked about his trashing the $565,000 house.

An alternative scenario would have been for Deane Beman to sit down with Daly and his representatives and quietly inform them that Daly would not be allowed to play on the tour again until he presented evidence of significant progress in an alcohol rehabilitation program. Many experts define that as an initial three to four weeks in a rehab facility, followed by ninety days of daily Alcoholics Anonymous–type meetings. Two and a half years after Daly had been hospitalized with alcohol poisoning while playing in a Hogan Tour event, the matter could finally be handled as firmly, yet discreetly, as every other instance of tour discipline that Beman managed. The media seldom discovered when a player had been fined by Beman, unless the player himself revealed it.

Instead, another press release was written, this one attributed jointly to Daly and Beman but coming from the tour office. It quoted Daly as saying: "I will check into an alcohol rehabilitation facility and will return to tournament play only when I am comfortable my life is in order." Beman was quoted as saying that Daly's withdrawal was voluntary, but that "we hope that a successful rehabilitation will lead to a return to the tour."

It was a document that was riddled with the veiled and conflicting agendas of dueling lawyers. Each side had layered sentences one upon another until they could all claim victory—particularly when it came to who was going to dictate the timing and circumstances of Daly's return. More interesting was that the tour office felt compelled to distribute information about what was, ultimately, a medical problem.

After almost two decades as tour commissioner, Deane Beman's proudest accomplishment on the job was not the abundance of money he had enabled thousands of golfers to earn, nor the real estate and merchandising empire he had created for the players through their administrative organization. It wasn't even the money that local tournaments were able to donate to charity as a result of the contributed services of ten of thousands of volunteer workers at PGA tournaments—which the tour publicized persistently. Nor was it the incalculable hours of entertainment professional golfers had provided to their fans.

What made Beman's chest swell more than anything was an astonishingly simple point: No sport was more respected for the conduct of its players than golf. Deane's boys—many of whom were over thirty—behaved themselves and never brought shame on their surrogate father. To a man who was the son of a public relations executive, whose upbringing had been financed by people looking to control their images, there was no higher compliment. His boys had done him proud.

Beman's paternalistic emphasis on player conduct would have outraged other professional athletes. They recognized their world-class athletic skills, honed by years of arduous practice, deserved more respect than that from the man they paid to run their sport. If on any given day any member of the tour could beat Deane Beman on the golf course, where did he get the right to then pat them on the head and tell them to just make sure they behaved themselves?

Beman was able to maintain this charade because it was intricately interwoven with the dirty little secret of social class and professional golf. For the first half of the twentieth century, most men who earned a living at golf did so by working for the wealthy at their country clubs. The club pros gave golf lessons to the members because they had more talent than the members, but they also repaired the members' clubs and cleaned their golf spikes because the members had more money and because they told them to.

Like the rest of the help the wealthy retained, golf pros at country clubs were supposed to vanish when they were not being of service. Most conspicuously, the club pros were prohibited from entering the clubhouses where the members socialized. If part of the allure of country club membership was the people one could meet, a corresponding component of it was whom one didn't have to encounter. It wasn't a coincidence that country clubs prominently displayed signs reading Private at the entrance to their long, sweeping driveways.

Young men who wanted to make golf a career—often to the consternation of their parents—apprenticed with club pros. One of the most important lessons they learned was never to forget that the members were of a different social class than they were. They were expected to be solicitous and friendly to the members but never familiar. If an apprentice had any ambition in life, he would be advised to be especially accommodating to the most highly placed members, as they were in a position to help a young man brighten his prospects in life.

Even as golf tournaments slowly became more popular, competitors were always identified as being either an amateur or a professional. The amateurs, who were often the sons of wealthy families or men in highly paid professions, were revered as being representative of the best of golf. The club professionals were seen as ne'er-do-wells or small-time hustlers, who smoked, drank, and cursed too freely. They were men a respectable girl would never marry.

The coming of stars such as Arnold Palmer, the broadcasting of tournaments, the increasing numbers of public golf courses, and even the dissipation of old money all contributed to the fading of these stereotypes. Yet, particularly among older golfers, the legacy of the professional as an interloper in the domain of the landed gentry was still evident.

Deane Beman was able to expand tournament purses exponentially by encouraging widespread corporate sponsorship of golf, but in doing so he trained his boys to grant the same deference to corporate America that their predecessors used to extend to country club members. PGA Tour golfers might not have to call a sponsor's CEO "Mr. Jones," but they were strongly encouraged to stop by his corporate hospitality tent on the grounds and do some grippin' and grinnin' after their round. Always the inducement was the same: "You never know what those powerful folks might be able to do for you." There were linen-covered tables galore in those tents, and they could yield bushels of crumbs to a man with the right attitude. Conversely, the quickest way to garner a fine was to publicly say something—anything—detrimental about a sponsor or host country club, even if what one said was true.

Forty years after country clubs started letting professional golfers into their clubhouses, there were still people in the game who thought this was an act of kindness on the part of the members. As socially inferior guests, it was then incumbent on the golfers to be on their best behavior, while the members themselves were only required to be civil. That was how Deane Beman had sold the PGA Tour to corporate America—saying, in essence, "You have my guarantee that if you sponsor a tournament, our boys will never embarrass you the way those tennis players would." By extension, he was saying: "Our boys know their place, and they are mighty grateful to have the work you're making possible."

That was why, when reports of John Daly's night of destruction hit newspapers nationwide, Beman concluded that it was more important to chastise Daly publicly than it was to quietly force him into rehab. Daly had acted like everyone's worst image of one of those 1950s club pros. Beman envisioned CEOs buzzing their administrative assistants, ordering them to find out whether this Daly boy had played in their tournament last year, and whether there was likely to be any trouble if he was to play this year. After Beman issued his press release, essentially flogging Daly in the town square at noon, the administrative assistants could buzz their CEOs back and say, "Don't worry, boss, Beman showed him good."

Daly had been deeply troubled by the news reports of his arrest, particularly the parts that said he had thrown Bettye against the wall and pulled her hair. He denied that in his press release, and he denied it in person to the people he discussed the case with, saying, "I never laid a hand on her. I'd wreck a house when I was mad, but I never hit anyone." He obsessed about this repeatedly until, as he was driving to the rehab facility near Tucson, Arizona, in early January, he had thoughts of committing suicide by crashing his car. He pulled over and called his best friend back home. "I feel like driving this car over a cliff," he said. "I never did anything wrong."

Somehow Daly resisted the urge and continued on to Sierra Tucson, a large treatment center that specialized in substance abuse. He hadn't given much thought to what the next three and a half weeks were going to be like, but he wasn't really worried about it. It was something he was being forced to do if he wanted to get back on the tour. He would play along, but it wasn't as though it were a big whoop or anything. He figured it would be similar to visiting a resort spa, where they put you on a special diet—stuff like that.

Daly got the first hint about how wrong he had been when they took him to the detox ward. Given the volume of alcohol he had been medicating himself with since he was a teenager, right up to the day he entered Sierra Tucson, Daly was going to go through three days of excruciating pain as his body was purged of booze. The staff would give him tranquilizers and megadoses of vitamins, along with plenty of fluids, to try to take the edge off, but there was only so much they could do.

Alcohol withdrawal for a heavy abuser was a process that involved weeping and the gnashing of teeth.

After detox, Daly spent the next ten days in a highly structured and activity-filled rehabilitation program. He was at the center by himself, while Bettye stayed at a hotel in town. Much of the treatment was directed at helping the patients learn new coping behaviors so they wouldn't turn to alcohol as a means of insulating themselves from the vagaries of life.

The part of the program Daly was anticipating most was a presentation by Thomas "Hollywood" Henderson, a former professional football player who had played linebacker for the Dallas Cowboys in three Super Bowls before his life was destroyed by a stupendous cocaine addiction that caused him to squander every penny he'd made in sports. It also led indirectly to his serving time in a maximum-security California prison on sexual battery and bribery charges involving two teenage girls.

Before Henderson arrived, Daly read an autobiography Henderson had published, called *Out of Control*. Although he had spent three years at the University of Arkansas, this was the first book Daly had read since his junior year at Helias High School, and he was quite taken by it.

In the book, Henderson talks, sometimes without remorse, about the endless party his life was while he was a sports star and cocaine addict. There was a seemingly interminable supply of women, sex parties, fur coats, and limousines—which accounted for Henderson acquiring the nickname Hollywood. He tells of his extended love affair with a working prostitute, whom he won away from an abusive pimp, and of craving the attention his football exploits brought him.

When Henderson began playing to the crowd, the Cowboys tried to steer the press away from him. Henderson responded by going directly to the press. He promoted himself by doing even more outrageous things on the football field. He once lost thirty-two pounds in three weeks by going on a malt liquor and salad diet in training camp. He had gambled when he was broke and couldn't afford to lose money. He was forced to go into rehab centers by his teams, and he would sneak out at night and get loaded. Then, thirty years old and a near derelict whose football career was over, he was arrested on the sex charges. The press, which had once been his friend, reported on the case, and Henderson was mortified. He thought about running off the road in his automobile to commit suicide.

When Henderson appeared at the rehab center, Daly sat in the front row of the audience and stared at him for an hour, hanging on his every word. Although Henderson, who had been free of drugs for ten years, was there as a fellow addict and addiction counselor—as well as a former professional athlete—Daly only stared. It was as if this were the U.S. Open of substance abuse and Henderson the Jack Nicklaus of addiction. Henderson understood it was Daly's move. When he didn't make one, Henderson left the facility without having said a word to him personally.

During the third week of the program, Jim and Lou Daly came in, much to the amazement of friends of the family. The Dalys weren't a clan that talked about this sort of thing much, but they wanted to do what they could for John. That week everyone learned that dysfunctional families, and those with substance abuse problems, don't often develop spontaneously. Harmful behavior and maladjustments usually get passed from generation to generation over decades, until one person, and then another, stands up and dedicates themselves to ending the cycle of pathology within their family. Jim Daly was moved enough that he decided to give up the booze as well.

As John's three and a half weeks of inpatient care were coming to an end, tournament organizers on the West Coast were wondering when Daly would be returning to competition. In recent years, the tour's marquee golfers had been overloading on the lucrative end-of-the-year TV events, then kicking back when the regular schedule resumed in California in January. The people who ran these events needed Daly to bolster their gate receipts.

Although hard figures were impossible to come by, it was conservatively estimated that Daly sold at least an extra five thousand tickets, at $20 and up per ticket, every day he played in a tournament. Over a four-day event, that was an additional $400,000 plus—not counting parking, beer, and hot dogs—that tournament organizers didn't want to forfeit. The television networks also drew additional viewers when Daly played, and they wanted him back on the course. Having Daly in rehab was like having an entire bank of slot machines incapacitated at a casino. Important people wanted the situation attended to with haste.

The guys at tour headquarters conferred on the predicament and decided that, hell, maybe they'd been a bit rash in making statements about successful rehabilitations. They weren't doctors. How did they know what a successful rehabilitation was—what with all this talk about one day at a time and everything? Attitude was the most important factor, and Daly had stayed in the facility for three weeks without bailing out. Besides, ultimately Daly had to accept responsibility for himself. Yeah, that was it. It was Daly's problem, not golf's.

Shortly after he left Sierra Tucson, Daly received a telephone call from Deane Beman's office. The commissioner wanted to talk to John, and the tour wanted to send a plane to pick him up, if that would be all right. Daly flew to Ponte Vedra and was told that it looked as though he was doing a good job of handling his alcohol problem. This was what the administration wanted to see, and if Daly chose to play at the following week's Phoenix Open, it would be fine with everyone at golf central.

This gave Daly two options. He could go into an aftercare program, where he would get up in front of strangers and talk about the multiple emotional traumas of his young life, which would cause him to experience for the first time the raw feelings he had previously suppressed with alcohol. He would cry profusely, and leave some of the meetings as numb as if someone had smashed him in the head with a baseball bat, as he recovered the ability to tolerate—and savor—human emotions.

The alternative was to go to a lush country club and play a game that he loved in the warm winter sun of the desert Southwest, while thousands of fans shouted hosannas at him and applauded his every move—when they weren't asking for his autograph or taking his picture. Each time he launched a ball from a tee, people would make appreciative sounds they never used at any other time in their lives, and they all would be directed at Daly, who would be made to feel like a king.

"Rehab was the greatest experience of my life," Daly said at his pretournament press conference at the Phoenix Open. "I've learned a lot of things about myself and my life, and I'm ready to get it on." So were the tour officials who were running the interview session. Before the meeting started, they announced that although they had once issued a press release as a sort of bon voyage card for Daly as he embarked upon his rehabilitation, suddenly they only wanted him to talk about golf.

As usual, Daly ignored what he was instructed to do and did what he wanted. In this case, that involved explaining the unique aftercare scheme he had devised for himself, one built as much on abstinence from AA meetings as from alcohol. Using a special form of logic, Daly tried to convince the reporters that attending too many aftercare meetings could be detrimental to his recovery. "It's a real slow program," he said. "I'm not too particular about hitting five or six AA meetings a week. But I will try to hit one every two weeks. I'll take it slow. I want to do it right." Using the same kind of thinking, Daly also told everyone that the police had dropped the charges against him in Colorado, although they were still very much outstanding. Demonstrating that he practiced denial as remarkably as he played golf, Daly had managed to convince himself that the court case was going to go away simply because he wanted it to.

Daly appeared on the course on Thursday feeling naked and unsure of what to expect from himself or his fans. He shot an excellent 69, and his fans were as boisterous as ever. Daly was hesitant about how to respond to them. He avoided eye contact and didn't smile much, as that seemed most comfortable. Friday he ballooned to a 74 and missed the cut.

It was the same pattern, only much, much worse the following week when he shot 74 then 86 at Pebble Beach, California. Fortunately he was playing with Fuzzy Zoeller, who was still his best—and, sometimes it seemed, only—friend on the tour. Fuzzy, along with Bettye and John's family and friends, had tried to talk John into getting professional help with his drinking for months before he hit bottom in Colorado, but he wouldn't listen to them. Because he genuinely liked John, Fuzzy kept being his friend, waiting for the day to come when something would force John to change—or at least begin to change.

Daly wasn't getting any follow-up help at all with his alcoholism, and every day he had strong cravings for beer. Some days he'd smell alcohol on people's breath and he'd be sorely tempted, especially as there was a new, or renewed, pressure in his life. Since he had left Sierra Tucson, things had been going quite badly between Bettye and him. At the end of February, John called his friend Rick Ross in Arkansas and said that he and Bettye were having problems again.

Ross wasn't at all surprised to hear this. He had thought

John and Bettye's days were numbered as soon as John started getting sober—that the dynamics of their relationship had been defined by John's drinking. If John wasn't drinking, the underpinnings of their marriage were drastically altered, and perhaps nonexistent. People got divorced all the time, so that wouldn't be a big deal. But there was something else that worried Ross. The press wrote about John all the time, but in actuality, both Bettye and John fought more viciously than any two people Ross had ever seen. He was worried about what might happen.

Head Shots

When golf coach Ray Hentges was introducing John Daly at the annual sports banquet at Helias High School during Daly's junior year, he told the audience of parents and student athletes that during some April in the future they were going to see Daly on TV wearing the green coat awarded to the winner of the Masters Tournament. Hentges said that in appreciation of Daly's talent; he selected the Masters because it is a prestigious event. People in the golf world started echoing Hentges after Daly won the 1991 PGA Championship, as the style of his game matches the idiosyncrasies of the Augusta National golf course perfectly. It favors golfers who are long off the tee and who have good short games, but penalizes wild shots only modestly because there is no high grass bordering the close-cropped fairways. In 1993 Daly almost proved them correct when, three months out of rehab, he finished tied for third at the tournament.

With everything he had on his mind, winning the Masters would have been even more miraculous than Crooked Stick. Daly was facing a hearing in Douglas County, Colorado, on May 25, and that was putting more than the normal nip in the cool mountain air outside Denver. It made Daly shiver momentarily every time he came home. That wasn't any way to live. Soon he was back in the housing market.

Even though their marriage was in trouble and they had occupied their place in Castle Rock for just nine months, the Dalys put that house up for sale and bought a 6,500-square-foot house in Isleworth, a posh gated community outside of Orlando, Florida, where other professional athletes lived. They planned to move in late April. Bettye was all for it, as she still thought John's not being able to play golf in December had contributed to the Christmas incident. It was to be their latest fresh start, and Bettye was steadfast in her belief that this time they were going to make it.

Nobody was seriously concerned that John Daly was going to go to jail on the assault charge if he was convicted. The odds were much stronger, though, that the judicial system might not be as indulgent as the PGA Tour had been concerning Daly's nonexistent aftercare program. Courts are much more likely to hand down mild probationary sentences to convicted first-time offenders when the defendants can demonstrate that they have taken steps to insure that their illegal behavior won't be revisited. Judges especially like it when the lawyers come into the courtroom with an entire remediation package in place, permitting the court to move on to the next case with a stern word, a sharp look, and a tap of the gavel.

John Daly was scheduled to play in the Houston Open during the first weekend in May, and Thomas Henderson, whose book and speech had affected Daly, lived in Austin. Henderson made his living now as an addiction counselor, and Daly called to ask if he would become Daly's rehabilitation sponsor—someone Daly could contact when he was under stress, feeling thirsty, and needed to talk. Henderson said sure, and came over to Houston to meet with John at the tournament.

Henderson arrived during the pretournament festivities,

just in time to witness how dramatically Daly had affected the world of golf. Tournament organizers had arranged a long-drive contest for early in the week. These were familiar competitions at tour stops, little crowd-pleasers to divert everyone, and to let the golfers pick up a few bucks, before the real tournament started. Normally they involved a handful of players and a modest purse, but this was Texas, and it was the post–Crooked Stick era.

The contest they arranged in Houston was intended to be a gunfight: John Daly versus Jim Dent, a big-hitting youngster against the longest driver on the Senior PGA Tour. The prize was winner take all: $80,000. You would have thought they were giving away free Stetsons at the golf course that day. Ten thousand hooting and hollering Texans showed up, intent on breaking up any congestion that might have accumulated in their lungs over the winter. In less time than it takes most people to eat breakfast, Daly beat Dent's best by twenty yards, pocketing enough dough to be able to tip the movers generously.

Back on the road again in late May, Daly arrived in Potomac, Maryland, where he had played well the previous year. He was so brimming with positive thinking that he sounded like Dale Carnegie's grandson. "My life is much more fun now," he told a press conference. "Everything in life seems to be so much easier. I'm doing more for myself in a positive way instead of doing things for everybody else. You've got to be happy with yourself before you can make other people happy. I'm definitely more happy with myself."

Daly's disposition dimmed considerably on Thursday when he shot a six-over 77. With his hearing in Colorado scheduled for the following Tuesday, Daly decided he didn't feel like playing golf anymore. He refused to sign his scorecard and got himself disqualified, and the event's hard-working organizers howled in pain at losing the biggest draw in an otherwise routine tournament field after one day.

The following week, the PGA Tour announced in a press release that Daly had pleaded guilty to a reduced charge of misdemeanor harassment in Douglas County. The original charge of third-degree assault was dismissed. The misdemeanor plea would be withdrawn entirely after Daly completed a counseling program for alcohol abuse—which would consist primarily of conversations with Thomas Henderson on an ad hoc basis.

Daly was greatly relieved to have the case behind him, but his life still had complications. One day he showed up at Rick Ross's place in Arkansas—just drove in without calling ahead or anything, which was unusual. "Rick," he said, "I can't handle this marriage anymore. She put the hammer on me to go into rehab, or she'd leave me and divorce me and all this stuff. She said it for months and months and months, and I finally made up my mind and did it.

"Now the shoe's on the other foot. I've been begging her for months and months to get some counseling. She has to deal with a lot of problems she has, but she won't do it. I told her she's either going to, or we're getting a divorce. She didn't do it, so I'm filing."

Ross didn't argue. He had thought for some time that John and Bettye had no choice but to end it. He believed they were bad for each other, that one of them was going to explode. The time bomb was there. They weren't able to communicate anymore except in raised voices, and John seemed to be getting stronger while Bettye was stuck in the wife-of-a-drinker mode. Ross had been waiting for one of them to blow a fuse and hurt the other one physically—not just emotionally or financially.

There was no question, however, that the divorce was going to cost Daly—now a twenty-seven-year-old multimillionaire—many millions of dollars over time, and leave Bettye far more prosperous than when she had entered the relationship, a mere three years earlier during the Macon Open. John's hefty income, and his having fathered a daughter with Bettye, would account for some of the coming redistribution of the wealth. But the killer inflationary element in the settlement equation would be what Marvin Mitchelson had anticipated eighteen months earlier: the hush money. Mitchelson had been right all along, he was just ahead of the curve.

During his first separation from Bettye four months after the PGA Championship, neither Daly nor his young advisers had fully appreciated the bonanza that Daly's career was about to become, so they weren't overly threatened. Everyone had caught on quickly since then, as Daly's income grew incessantly. Plus Bettye's negotiators now had another year and a half's worth of private-life details that John might want to have die with the marriage. He had taken all the PR hits in recent months that he was going to be able to stand for a while. Stifling Bettye would be mandatory. As Marvin Mitchelson had known, and as the people now affiliated with the case had learned, silence could be an extraordinarily expensive commodity on the open market. But for someone in Daly's position, it was the domestic-relations equivalent of the cost of doing business.

With all of this to distract him, Daly wasn't setting records on the golf course. At a tournament in Westchester County, New York, in June—the one sponsored by Buick that he'd missed the previous year after deplaning in Denver—he shot a 74 and an 82 and snapped both his driver and his three-wood in half before finishing nine holes of the second round. The U.S. Open was the following week, and Daly put in an emergency call to Rick Ross to ask if he could fly up to help him restore the symmetry to his swing.

The Open was being played in northern New Jersey in the midst of an extended heat wave. Temperatures in the Northeast were routinely passing 100 degrees. Daly arrived at the historic Baltusrol Golf Club and discovered that no one was interested in his personal problems, which Daly had kept private, or his deteriorating golf game. The crowd at the U.S. Open had only one thing on its mind. The course featured a 630-yard par five hole, and no human had ever reached the green in two shots. Before they left that week, those people wanted to see Daly put his second shot on the putting surface.

Daly was working with Ross on the practice range, trying to get his game in order, and all anyone else wanted to talk about was the seventeenth hole and whether Daly thought he could do it. Other than Ross and Daly, no one else cared very much whether Daly won the tournament or even got into contention. Finally Daly gave in and made the seventeenth the focus of his week as well. "We may not play very well," he told his caddie, "but at least we'll make history."

It happened on Friday. After hitting a drive of more than 325 yards, Daly had about 300 yards remaining to the hole. He crucified his ball with a one-iron, and it landed short of the green, bounced onto it, and rolled forty-five feet beyond the cup. Daly wasn't near the top of the leaderboard, but he swiftly became the main topic of conversation at the tournament, much to the consternation of some of the other golfers, who thought they were playing in a major, not attending a long-drive contest.

Contributing to the ill will was the eight-page profile of Daly that had run in *Sports Illustrated* (the locker room refrain: "And he's only won two tournaments!") the week before. Daly told writer Rick Reilly, "I know there's a lot of guys who would love to see me fail. Well, good, let 'em. I'm glad." Perhaps it shouldn't have come as a surprise, then, when Daly's playing partner, Payne Stewart, said he hadn't noticed Daly's historic shots on the seventeenth, as he had been too busy paying attention to his own game—even if most of the spectators and the media weren't.

Daly tied for thirty-third at the U.S. Open, and did some globe-trotting before winding up back in Memphis for the St. Jude tournament at the end of July. His old hometown was about to become his third city of residence in seven months. It was a given that Bettye was getting the Orlando house, and John wasn't about to move back to Castle Rock.

The St. Jude was one of Daly's payback tournaments. They had repeatedly given him sponsor exemptions when he was an unknown, and because so few people had helped Daly along the way, he didn't forget those who had. Memphis also considered him an adopted native son, and the golf fans there were even more vocal in their support for him than people were at other events—if that was possible.

Many spectators were running from hole to hole at the tournament on Friday, only interested in seeing Daly's tee shots. They didn't care about his second shots or putts, or any balls hit by any other golfers. This caused tidal waves of movement on the course as people scampered for the best viewing positions.

There was a crosswalk on the ninth fairway, two hundred yards down from the tee. Course marshals opened it, when there weren't golfers teeing off, allowing people to move about. When Daly came to the ninth tee, the crosswalk over-flowed with spectators, and Daly got tired of waiting for the marshals to close the passageway. With the crosswalk full, he teed up a ball and let it fly, right over the heads of everyone on the course. As people ducked and covered their faces, the ball carried beyond them before hitting the ground. "I just figure when I'm ready to hit, I'm going to hit," Daly said later when reporters asked him why he had done such a thing.

Daly finished up Friday one shot off the lead, and that meant pandemonium at the course on Saturday. With the sum-mer heat wave unabated, people poured through the gates on Saturday, casting off money everywhere so their wallets would be lighter to carry in the sopping humidity. With John Daly near the top of the leaderboard, the tournament set third-round sales records for everything—tickets, parking, refreshments, and souvenirs.

By the end of the day, Daly was five shots out of the lead and no longer a factor, but it was okay because he had been replaced near the top of the heap by Fuzzy Zoeller. Zoeller was battling Nick Price, whose wife was about to have a baby. If Price's wife called, he was leaving. Ironically, the last tournament Price dropped out of because his wife was about to give birth was the 1991 PGA Championship. Price's spot had been taken by John Daly.

At his press conference on Saturday night, reporters asked Zoeller if he was tempted to call Price, imitate his wife, and say that her time was at hand. "No," Zoeller said, "but I might take him out and buy him a few beers. I don't think the boy is drinking nearly enough."

Daly also had another consolation for losing his way at the St. Jude. Paulette Dean, the "Classic" girl from the Hope Chrysler Classic, was about to come back into his life. They had talked on the phone. John told her it was over with Bettye and invited her down to Tennessee. He said to bring a suitcase. Paulette said she'd be there.

Paulette had made a favorable impression on John's friends with the way she had handled herself when she and John broke up and he went back to Bettye. *Golf World* magazine had tracked Paulette down and asked her how she felt about everything. "I have no hard feelings," she said. "We had different things we wanted to do in life. I wish him and Bettye the best. He's the father of the child. He's where he needs to be."

There was some apprehension about her not being a southerner—and being a California girl at that—but it had passed. The consensus was that she was real and down-to-earth, and that she was more interested in John as a person than as a provider. It also did not escape notice that it was John's first lady friend in ages who was younger than he.

All of this was supposed to be a secret. John's people were telling him to keep his mouth battened until they massaged the numbers with Bettye's people. John couldn't help himself, though. Sometimes yielding to impulse was as involuntary for him as breathing was for everyone else. As he was approaching the first tee at St. Jude on Sunday, where he would be introduced, he told them to say he was John Daly from Memphis, Tennessee—not Orlando. Bobby Hall, the golf writer from the Memphis paper, questioned Daly about this, but Daly wouldn't answer him.

John showed better control when *USA Today*'s Steve Hershey ran an item several weeks later noting that Daly's marriage was in trouble. John told him, "It's tough. It's day-to-day. I've done everything I can."

Bettye said she was devastated: "I don't know what to say. I just hope we can work through this and get on with our lives." Bettye was heavily into denial, as John had filed for divorce and cleared his stuff out of the house. She probably didn't need to know that he was signing a lease on a place for him and Paulette in suburban Memphis.

A couple of weeks later Daly was playing at a non-PGA charity tournament in Portland, Oregon. It was an annual event that Bettye and he had first attended in 1991—right after the PGA Championship and the International in Castle Rock. A bunch of golfers from the tour were there, and Daly was involved in an exhibition before a large gallery. Daly started getting bored, the way that he could, and then he got fidgety.

He wasn't thinking too clearly, but whatever it was that he was thinking, it wasn't far removed from what had been in his head in the spring of 1982, when he was standing in Brad Struttmann's front yard, with the guys from the golf team looking on, as he gazed down the street to see the team's practice course beckoning him. Same thing when the people were moving through the overloaded crosswalk in Tennessee like ducks in a shooting gallery.

It always had to do with getting their attention, because why else would you fire a golf ball over their heads like a bullet? What you wanted them to see was how superbly you could hit the ball. You could ask them to pay you mind, but if they didn't, now, that hurt. It was a far safer thing to force them to look, then shrug as if it hadn't been for display.

In the middle of the exhibition at the tournament in Portland, John Daly aimed a ball away from the open field and toward the heads of the spectators who were sitting on a hill.

"No!" Brad Struttmann seemed to be yelling through time, from a decade before in Jefferson City. *"Are you crazy? Don't. John, stop."*

Daly drove the ball over the spectators, and everyone stared at him in appalled silence. What was wrong with this man? What vital component had been left on the bench during his assembly? What could you tell your children when they witnessed behavior like this?

That was August. On the first of October, during his front nine at the Southern Open in Pine Mountain, Georgia, he put two balls in the water on one hole, then bogeyed two of the next three holes. Daly's rage slopped over the top so quickly that he walked off the course after nine holes, loaded his car, and drove away, offering no explanation for his actions. Later in the month, at the World Match Play Championship in Virginia Water, England, he flung his putter across the green after missing a short putt. Finally, on November 5, Daly was playing badly during a tournament at the Kapalua Bay resort on the Hawaiian island of Maui. Again, he picked up his ball and got himself disqualified from a tour event.

Half the denizens of the world of professional golf were convinced John Daly was drinking again, although no one had spied him with a bottle in his hand. There were two possibilities. He had become a dry drunk—a former drinker who continues the same behavior patterns while sober. Or, he was drinking again.

The one certainty was that—if only subconsciously—Daly was looking for a showdown with Deane Beman. When one flagrant violation of tour regulations didn't produce it, Daly quickly followed up with another, then another. The Kapalua incident occurred during a Friday afternoon round at a relatively obscure end-of-the-year tournament. It could have been handled with one more fine and letter of admonition. Beman was already penalizing Daly so regularly that John could have confused his payments to the tour with deposits to a Christmas club savings account.

But Daly had adroitly pushed Beman to the brink, to where it seemed that every week Beman was setting his jaw and shaking his head over another Daly bulletin from the front. Now the commissioner was going to give Daly what he wanted—he was going to push back. He sent word for Daly and his people not to leave Hawaii. They had a compulsory appointment with Beman for Sunday, and it wasn't for brunch.

16

Deane's Retreat

For all his zeal for confrontation and his reputation for invincibility, it was a chastened Deane Beman who would be meeting with John Daly on Maui. Only four months away from his twentieth anniversary on the job, Beman was a man who had been given the opportunity to experience the bitter-sweetness of human vulnerability during the past year. Over the first three-quarters of his reign, the tour's growth had been so electrifying and lucrative that Beman had enjoyed a honeymoon period of epic proportions. The novelty of professional golfers making that kind of money was so delightful that any dissent among the rank and file was giggled off.

The purses inevitably peaked, just as the boys had acquired a taste for those huge annual increases. They grew disgruntled, talked among themselves, and occasionally went public. Once the players put Beman in play, he became fair game for the golf press. *Golf Digest*, which, like all enthusiast magazines, relies heavily on cooperation from tour players for instructional articles, ran a blistering three-part critique of the commissioner in 1992, with the first article entitled "Can Beman

Survive?" A number of golfers criticized Beman on the record in the series, particularly for his bullying style.

Beman's adversaries had been emboldened by the highly visible albatross the commissioner was lugging around—a massive, unwinnable lawsuit that was swallowing tour money as quickly as Beman could sign the checks. A number of veteran golfers had been complaining in recent years that modern golf equipment had become too much of a factor in the game—that it was diminishing the value of skill and talent in winning golf tournaments. Although there was no hard evidence to prove this, Beman decided he was going to make it the legacy issue of his administration. He preemptively banned a certain style of Ping golf clubs from the PGA Tour, saying they allowed golfers to put too much spin on errant drives that had run off the fairway.

Ping's founder, Karsten Solheim, was an eccentric engineer who had developed a novel putter in his home workshop decades earlier, then traveled to golf tournaments and sold them to professional golfers out of his car. Using the same approach with full sets of golf clubs, he had gone on to create one of the largest golf equipment companies in the United States. His success was an outgrowth of his ties with the PGA Tour. His expensive, top-of-the-line clubs virtually sold themselves to amateurs, with only minimal marketing, because they were the same clubs the pros used to win tournaments. Banning Ping clubs from the tour would destroy the unique marketing approach that was the company's foundation.

The willingness to cavalierly blow someone else's painstakingly nurtured company out of the water without breaking stride was vintage Beman. But the commissioner had been dealing with Fortune 500 CEOs for so long that he had lost the ability to distinguish between a company man and a company owner. Before Deane Beman drove Karsten Solheim out of business, Beman was going to know that he had been in a fight. After a protracted and highly visible legal battle, Solheim forced Beman into a humiliating surrender that, between the settlement and legal fees, involved millions of dollars of the tour's money. And Ping clubs were permitted back on the tour. It was a monumental and total defeat for Beman.

With Beman's abrasive personal style, he had a limited number of close friends in reserve to defend him against the backlash that developed after the settlement. Nonetheless, having consistently paid himself more than his top players were earning in tournament winnings, Beman was an independently wealthy, fifty-five-year-old man with a younger second wife. He had done his empire building and he was financially secure, but now the perimeter walls had been breached. The only realistic option was to prepare to go into exile from the tour.

The Deane Beman who met with John Daly on November 7 was a man whose shoulders were no longer constantly hunched. He didn't have anything to prove anymore—but he probably couldn't have mustered the authority to prove anything even if he had wanted to. This allowed Beman to talk to Daly as a concerned authority figure rather than a potentate. Daly, who had arrived expecting the threatening fingerpointer of old, was flabbergasted. Nothing infuriated Daly faster than men who tried to order him around. When Beman acted decently toward him, Daly was actually able to hear what he had to say.

Daly was going to be suspended; there wasn't any question about that. But this time Beman was able to explain to Daly that it was in the best interest of both Daly and the tour for him to take some time off to get himself together. He pointed out that people paid good money, and sometimes traveled great distances, to see Daly play in a tournament. He could no more walk off the course in the middle of a round than an actor could leave the stage during a play—not and expect people to come back. To scare him, Beman told Daly that the suspension was for an indefinite time, but he didn't raise his voice or threaten him, which were Daly's psychological melt-down buttons. The meeting went better than people had a right to expect, and Beman even managed to convince Daly that he needed the tour but the tour didn't need Daly—which was patently false.

Beman called a press conference and came out sounding like a mail-order humanitarian. John Daly, he said, "needs support, he needs understanding, and he needs professional help. John has made great strides in the last year, but he has additional challenges to conquer. Stopping drinking is only half the battle. Getting back into the mainstream of life and dealing with people and situations, that can only be done with aftercare. John skipped that, and he's having difficulty functioning in everyday life with sobriety."

Beman announced the indefinite suspension and said it required Daly to seek professional counseling. Beman took that to mean additional inpatient or outpatient care at a rehabilitation center, while Daly thought he had agreed to talk to Thomas Henderson more frequently. Daly couldn't stand those sessions where he had to listen to other people talking about the horrendous things they had done when they were drunk—perhaps because the stories hit too close to home.

Beman had suspended Daly from PGA Tour events, but he couldn't stop Daly from playing anywhere he wanted outside the United States. With a junket to Mexico already scheduled for the following week, Daly went there to play. Reporters normally would have paid this tournament little regard, but it was going to be Daly's first appearance since his suspension, and they were betting—and hoping—he would have something to say.

Daly played an exhibition match at Mexico City's Club de Gold La Hacienda, before his planned participation in the Mexican Open. When he met with reporters at the club, he had one overriding concern. Just as he had insisted repeatedly that he had never hit Bettye in Colorado, he was adamant that he had not resumed drinking since leaving rehab.

"That's the thing I want to stress the most," he said. "I am not drinking again. I definitely am not. No, sir. When Deane said that part of the suspension had to do with me getting counseling, people thought that meant drinking. It doesn't. I'll go get tested . . . if people want me to do that."

Daly said his erratic behavior during the fall hadn't been the result of an alcohol relapse, but came from the difficulties of sobriety. "You know, things bother you more," he said. "It's the first time I've felt pain."

After finishing more than twenty shots off the lead in the Mexican Open, Daly resisted the urge to collect hefty appearance fees around the world, which would have violated the spirit of his suspension. He went to the Palm Springs area of California, where Paulette was from, and bought a condo near the Mission Hills Country Club, where he engaged in marathon practice sessions. Whereas Bettye had previously assigned him to play tennis as alcohol-avoidance busywork, John took charge of the situation himself now. He hit golf balls until he created new calluses on his hands, even after having been a professional golfer for over six years. It was as if he were a teenager again, when his friends were working or out on dates and John was out on the golf course, preparing for his career. He lost himself in the simple rhythms of hitting the same shots repeatedly, and because he was doing it by himself, and for himself, it seemed to bleed down his reservoir of stress.

John and Paulette made a trip east to do some work for John's sponsors, then detoured to the University of Virginia in Charlottesville to see Bob Rotella, a sports psychologist. Deane Beman was leaning on Daly to get counseling, and Daly wanted to determine if Rotella might be able to help him with his problems. Rotella had worked with a number of professional golfers, both male and female, as well as other professional athletes, many of whom had been generous in their praise of how effective he was in helping them improve their athletic performance.

Because Rotella has a doctorate, and the word "psychologist" is in his title, many people in professional sports without wide experience in these matters assume that Rotella is going to ask them about their childhood and how they felt about their parents. Nothing could be further from the truth. The operant word in Rotella's title is *sports*. It's his job, and his only job, to help his clients improve the mental aspects of their athletic performance—period.

You go to a sports psychologist because you want to run faster or make more free throws—often by improving your concentration. Professional athlete or not, going to a sports psychologist to improve your personal life is about as effective as going to a psychiatrist to improve your golf game—they are professionals who do entirely different things.

Rotella is the son of a barber who raised three sons. Each had enough drive to overcome their modest origins and earn a doctorate. Bob had spent time working with handicapped children. Not surprisingly, he is a strong believer in the can-do spirit and in not dwelling on the past. His theory of how to find happiness in life reflects this: Wake up every morning thinking about the wonderful things you are going to do that day. Go to sleep each night thinking about the wonderful events of the past day and the wonderful things you will do tomorrow. Anyone who does that will be happy.

Daly poured his story out to Rotella over the better part of a working day, filling in all the details, which included very few occasions on which he had gone to sleep thinking about the wonderful events of his day. Daly was having some problems getting behind the idea that his attitude was the source of his difficulties, what with his having consumed over a bottle of liquor a day at some points in his life, and what with the latent rage that always seemed to be loosely tethered within him.

Daly said he was often so overwhelmed by his personal problems that he thought about them on the golf course. Rotella told him he better cut that out if he wanted to win more golf tournaments. Daly said that, as a result of his background, if he didn't play especially well most of the time, he felt like he was wasting his talents. Rotella told him that it was a shame that his past had been so difficult, but that he better get over it if he wanted to become a better golfer.

Rotella told him what he told all the golfers he worked with, regardless of their background or personality: Work on your short game, stay focused on every shot, and never hit the ball until you are ready. Daly said okay, and pretty soon they started running out of things to talk about, what with the events of Daly's past not being worth going into too much, because it was, after all, just the past. The future—that was where you wanted to be directed. If you saw the future as being inexorably linked to the past, well, that was pretty much your problem.

Other than talking to Thomas Henderson on the phone quite a bit, that was it for John Daly and alcohol counseling. Daly had been out of action for nearly three months, and the tournament sponsors were getting vociferous in their cries to bring him back. Finally Deane Beman set up a meeting with Daly in Palm Springs for the middle of February, after which Beman announced that he had decided to let Daly return to action during the second week of March, at the Honda tournament. As a condition of his return, Daly promised to seek alcohol counseling.

Two weeks after their conversation, on the twentieth anniversary of his having become commissioner, Beman announced his retirement. He was under contact to the tour for almost two additional years, until December 1995, but he said he wanted out as soon as a replacement could be found. The players thanked Beman for all he had done for them, but they didn't try to convince him to stay.

Daly arrived in Florida for the Honda tournament and came to a pretournament press conference surrounded by an entourage of sponsors, agents, and Paulette. "I'm starting a whole new career right here," he said, brimming with confidence and a new philosophy. "I've got a lot of personal things off my mind. I have a clear mind now. I'm just going to forget about the past and concentrate on golf."

Indeed, something seemed to have changed. Appearing in his first tournament in four months, Daly finished tied for fourth place. "I focused on every shot and played my heart out," Daly said. "If I was wearing a hat right now, I'd take it off to myself. I'm real proud."

As Daly was talking to the reporters in the front of the room, Paulette was chatting with some at the back, in a manner much different from that favored by Bettye. "Since he stopped drinking, he's a different person," she said. "Before, he was so unpredictable. He's a lot more mellow now. He doesn't get angry anymore, and I think he has a lot better sense of humor. I like him much better this way."

In his excitement about playing well, Daly apparently got confused for a minute. Deane Beman had told Daly he had to get more counseling as a condition of his return from suspension, but Daly was telling the reporters there weren't any conditions at all attached to his return. Oh, well, the new commissioner would be too preoccupied to find out about that deal anyway.

The roller coaster of John Daly's life, having struggled up another peak, descended at free-fall speed in the following weeks. In his next four tournaments, he finished twenty-first in one, missed two cuts, and finished forty-eighth at the Masters. Every professional's golf game comes and goes, but at the Masters Daly had a relapse of behavior he had been told was unacceptable. For most of the week Daly was so distraught about his performance that he refused to talk to reporters.

Later in April, Daly rolled into a tournament in North Carolina that had a reputation for rowdy galleries and high-volume beer concessions. Arriving as he was, in the midst of an extended slump, this would normally be a time of great temptation for Daly. Now that he wasn't drinking, Daly had to identify some substitute behavior to release the tension.

When Daly arrived in Greensboro, he told himself that if he didn't shoot par or better during his first round, he was going to shave his head. After recording a 78 that day, he got out the razor. He wasn't playing well, so he figured that he might as well laugh and have a good time.

He showed up at the course on Friday morning wearing a hat to disguise his handiwork and to protect his scalp against the early spring chill. But Daly couldn't resist doffing his cap on the first tee for his fans. He had done this for them, after all. The crowd erupted when they saw Daly's head. No one in the history of golf had ever done anything like this. Shaved heads were largely the province of black men who played basketball and football and who boxed. Once again, John Daly had set tongues clicking in the locker room. The bald scalp did wonders for his spectator bonding but nothing for his golf game. Daly shot an 84 on Friday and missed the cut by a mile.

News—and pictures—of Daly's haircut preceded him to the next tournament at The Woodlands, a golf development north of Houston. Daly's game suddenly came back, and when he was in a position to possibly win on Sunday, guys with flesh-colored skullcaps came pouring in through the turnstiles as though the tournament organizers were holding auditions for a toupee commercial. The parking lots were overflowing, and at the gates they were turning away people who had $20 bills clenched in their hands. Daly finished tied for seventh at the tournament, behind a clutch of golfers the guys in the skullcaps wouldn't remember.

It had been almost a year since John had filed for divorce

from Bettye, but the case wasn't going anywhere. Every time it looked as if it was going to go through, Bettye's lawyers would come up with another delaying tactic. Some of it was strategic, aimed at keeping the pressure on during negotiations, but Bettye also seemed to be holding out hope for a reconciliation, which everyone associated with John knew wasn't going to happen.

During the first week of May, while John was preparing for a tournament outside Atlanta, he suddenly discovered that his motion to schedule visitations with his daughter, Shynah, was going to be heard in Orlando the next morning. With his aversion to flying still strong, Daly drove the 450 miles to Orlando, attended the hearing—where a visitation schedule was agreed upon—and returned to the suburbs of Atlanta, arriving after midnight.

Even with his shaved head, Daly seemed to bring a seriousness of purpose back with him from Orlando and onto the first tee the next morning. He often ignored his fans' pleas for him to wallop the ball with his driver, instead using irons off the tees at the narrow and hilly Atlanta Country Club course. He shot for the middle of the greens instead of for the flag and tried to concentrate more. He knew he was in a slump, and instead of trying to blast out of it, he was carefully working his way out. At the end of the day he was three shots off the lead.

Using the same strategy on Friday, he shot a 64 and claimed a two-shot lead. People in the pressroom were wondering what had gotten into Daly. He appeared calm and patient on the course, and he was playing percentage golf. With no indications to the contrary, he was apparently doing all of this without the insulating effects of nightly infusions of alcohol.

Golf fans in Georgia weren't reading about Daly's new style of play in the fine print of their local newspapers on Saturday morning. They were looking at the headlines—"Daly Leads BellSouth Classic by 2"—and lacing on their walking shoes. Half of Atlanta seemed to be at the course, and in Daly's gallery, as he maintained his two-shot lead on Saturday.

On Sunday Daly came to the first tee swaddled in the midst of fourteen marshals, who had been assigned to protect him from his adoring fans. He had said at the B.C. Open that winning his second tournament had been harder than winning his first. Now he faced a much more complex challenge. Could he overcome his natural doubts and fears, without alcohol, and withstand the brutal pressure of the last nine holes on Sunday to win the golf tournament?

It appeared as though Daly was going to turn the tournament into a rout, as he quickly ran his lead up to four shots. Then, like a novice high-wire walker, he made the potentially lethal mistake of looking down. He realized he was on his way to winning a PGA tournament without the fortification of alcohol, and he wasn't sure he had worked up a self-image to handle that.

He began playing sloppy golf, picking up a stroke on one hole only to lose it on the next. Most often, though, he lost strokes. By the time he came to the eighteenth tee, Daly had fallen into a tie for the lead.

The eighteenth was a par five hole, but it was a tricky one. The smart play was to hit an iron off the tee. That was the kind of golf that had gotten him into the lead but which had also caused him to lose it. If he were to rip a classic Long John Daly drive down the fairway, and he didn't slice it, he could birdie the hole easily and probably avoid a playoff. What would it be, Dr. Jekyll or Mr. Hyde?

It sounded like a cannon had been fired when the throng at the eighteenth hole saw Daly reach for his driver. This was the John Daly the spectators had come to the golf course to see, not some namby-pamby percentage shooter. If truth be told, the fans probably liked Daly better as a drinker. They'd accept sobriety to a point, but only if it didn't turn him into some damn wimp.

Daly blew a 320-yarder down the fairway, followed by a 172-yard eight-iron into a sand trap off the green. He exploded the ball out of the trap, dropped a four-foot putt, and the tournament was his.

Observing this from the side of the eighteenth green was a friend from Dardanelle, Don Cline, the hospital administrator Daly had often turned to when he was in trouble—or deadly drunk. Cline was crying tears of relief before Daly could retrieve his ball from the cup. "He's going to be all right," Cline said. "This shows it. He's really grown up."

"I never got nervous playing golf when I drank," Daly said at the awards ceremony, his voice husky. "But I'm still shaking now. It's a great win, knowing how hard I worked before I came back out. I can honestly say it's the first time I've won a PGA tournament in a sober manner. It's a great feeling knowing I can win sober."

Daly's eyes got watery, and he paused for a moment. Then, sounding like a little boy whom the people in charge had always scolded and called a screwup, Daly served notice that he expected recognition for having behaved himself. "I'm proud I'm doing the right things I'm supposed to do to win," he said.

17

Glory Days

 John Daly fever was epidemic among golf fans in the aftermath of his Atlanta victory. Fuzzy Zoeller had Daly up to an exhibition match he staged at a course near his New Albany, Indiana, home in late May. Arnold Palmer and Chi Chi Rodriguez, two huge crowd favorites from the senior tour, and Hubert Green from the main tour, were also at the match, but no one seemed to notice. The spectators' secondary interest that day was obtaining Daly's autograph or his picture, but what they wanted mostly was what everybody else wanted—to see him bore holes into the horizon with golf balls. "I'm just an ugly country boy from Arkansas who plays golf," Daly told reporters with a straight face after he had escaped the hordes. "I always dreamed of having the crowd on my side, everybody cheering for me. I just never dreamed it would be this big."

When the folks at Wilson Sporting Goods started thinking about how big Daly had become, they decided he could be the solution to a distressing dilemma they were facing. Wilson was an eighty-year-old middle-sized company that had spent recent years on corporate life support after having been mowed down by newcomers to the sporting goods field such as Nike and Reebok. Wilson's Finnish parent company, the Amer Group, had hired turnaround experts to slash the staff by 26 percent, which restored profitability. Then, after leaving the company without a CEO for five months, Amer Group hired John Riccitiello in November of 1993. He was Wilson's fifth president in four years.

Riccitiello was only thirty-five and had never worked in sporting goods—but that was the idea. They wanted somebody young and unjaded. He had impressed people with the innovative marketing work he had done with jazzy operations such as Häagen-Dazs and PepsiCo. With an eye toward Nike's "Just Do It" advertising campaign and their frequent high-profile use of sports celebrities, Amer Group told Riccitiello to recast Wilson from a snoozing grandpappy into a hot, sexy young thing whose products people would view as primary to a get-down life.

Golf products accounted for almost half of Wilson's revenue, but the company was being overtaken in this area by competitors who had more innovative equipment, which amateur golfers love and spend freely on. Riccitiello decided to spring for research to develop new clubs and balls that would give weekend golfers an edge. Then came his specialty—he was going to market the hell out of the new stuff the tech guys whipped up.

No sooner had Riccitiello shared this vision with his associates than the nucleus of his golf endorsement program skipped. Wilson had John Daly under contract for a reported $1 million a year with bonuses, but the mainstay of their marketing program for 1994 was going to be golfer Payne Stewart, who had been under contract. Before Wilson could get Stewart's signature on a new deal, however, he signed with the enemy: Spalding. Losing Stewart was tough in and of itself. Even stickier was what it said to people in the industry—Wilson might have a young stud as a CEO, but the company remains so moribund it can't even retain its celebrities.

This happened in December 1993, while Wilson's other star golfer, John Daly, was on suspension from the tour, leaving Wilson with no one to feature in its drop-dead new golf marketing campaigns. It might have been just as well, what with Daly always pulling something psycho. Then what should happen but John Daly's arising from his rehab bed like an apparition and winning a golf tournament sober—and bald. You had the recovery thing, the punky postmodern naked head, the angst. Handled right, this could be totally edgy. It could work. It could really work.

The people at Wilson ripped up Daly's million-dollar-a-year contract, which had two years left on the meter, and got on the phone. They told Daly's people to hire themselves some dump trucks—the big mothers with the air brakes—so they could stuff the beds with money. They shut down construction jobs to get enough vehicles. By the time all the grunting and heavy lifting were done, Daly's new deal with Wilson topped out at $30 million over ten years.

Only five years earlier, John and his first wife, Dale, had fought over whether both of them could afford to travel to golf tournaments and over how much they could spend on hotels. Only five years before that, John had transferred out of Helias High School during the middle of his senior year and moved to Dardanelle in order to lower his partial tuition at the University of Arkansas. Through it all, he always believed he would be able to make his living on the PGA Tour. Now, at twenty-eight, when everything was computed, his annual income was going to put him in the top ten of all professional golfers in the world. John Daly had so much money he could stock Lake Dardanelle with hundred-dollar bills rather than trout.

Daly was always circumspect about his riches. He might

sometimes buy houses the way other people bought groceries, and he gambled, but he did these things relatively quietly for someone with his visibility. He never went out of his way to impress anyone with his loot, and there was a reason for that.

As he was fond of describing himself, John Daly was just a good ol' country boy. He knew that if you cut too much firewood during the fall and stacked it right alongside the house, everybody who came down the road was going to see that pile there. Out of normal curiosity, they were going to wonder where you got the wood, and what you were going to do with it. After a while they'd get to thinking it probably wasn't right that you had more firewood than they did and that you were flaunting it so. They'd get to wondering if maybe you hadn't done something crooked to get it. Pretty soon people would be agreeing among themselves that you had acquired the wood by nefarious means, and that it gave them the right to come by and borrow some while you were off tending to your land.

That's why, when reporters started asking Daly about his new contract with Wilson, he told them, sure enough, it did run ten years, but you know, he couldn't rightly say how much it was for. He hadn't even paid any mind to the money. He was just right proud that Wilson believed in him that way, and he hoped he could be with such an upstanding company for his entire career.

All of this was fine and good, except that the other parties to the transaction were impatient for the world to learn about the deal. Wilson was trying to establish that it was a player— that Payne Stewart hadn't jumped because Wilson was cheap and provincial. By fire-hosing Daly with money, Wilson was making a statement. It was saying it could afford to be reckless with the bucks, so consumers and competitors would think that this was a way-cool company this young dude was running here.

The people at Daly's management company also couldn't

mind if other golfers on the tour began to scratch their heads and ask: "What is wrong with this picture? My agent isn't getting *me* anywhere near this kind of money for endorsements." As an inevitable side effect of all this visibility, though, guys in the locker room were going to be mentioning to each other that $30 million worked out to $10 million for each of Daly's tournament victories to date.

Even as Daly cringed, there were leaks galore to the press about the Wilson deal. In case these weren't completely effective in disseminating the news, Wilson called a press conference at the U.S. Open to herald the contract—without mentioning the numbers, wink, wink—to the hundreds of international media representatives present. Daly really didn't think this was a good idea, boasting and leaving his deposit slips sitting out on the table, but people kept telling him he had to do it—which only made it worse. He was also signing a new contract with Reebok, and they weren't blabbing about it in the media. Ultimately, Daly compromised by showing up late for the Wilson press session and clearing out fast, but the contract numbers had already been widely circulated by then.

Nearly a year had passed since John had filed for divorce from Bettye, but the case was far from resolved. Bettye's negotiators were following the sports pages the way brokers monitor stocks on Wall Street. Every time John won a tournament—which is not to say signed a $30 million contract—calculators started smoking and spreadsheet software blinked out forecasts. John's income projections were outpacing increases in the Dow Jones industrial average by twentyfold, causing Bettye's camp to adopt a new slogan for negotiating the divorce settlement: What's the hurry?

John was infuriated by all of this because, quite simply, Bettye had him. The moment the divorce was finalized she would become John Daly's ex-wife, someone whose name, even with its distinctive spelling, would quickly slip from people's minds. John was going to keep on riding the gilded carousel of the PGA Tour, where the notes of the pipe organ were always pleasantly round. John desperately wanted to establish a regular visitation schedule with his daughter, Shynah, but Bettye had his plea bargain in Colorado to argue against that.

To make matters even more inflammatory, he couldn't utter a sound in public about what was going on. His lawyers had slapped a total embargo on talk about the case, knowing Bettye's lawyers would use any defamatory stories about her the way football coaches used bad-mouthing quotes from opposing players. They'd pin them on the bulletin board to provide table-thumping inspiration during the battle. Since he couldn't, as Bob Rotella had suggested, simply forget about all of this, it left John with one option—he could stew.

He left his U.S. Open press conference and missed the cut in the tournament, shooting an 81 on Friday. In Hartford, Connecticut, the following week, he developed a mysterious pain in his lower back and went to see a doctor. For years people had said that Daly's extremely long swing should be causing him back trouble, but it never had. The doctor couldn't find anything. On Sunday at the tournament, Daly failed to notice his playing partner had made a mistake in recording Daly's score. Daly signed the incorrect scorecard and was disqualified from the tournament after it had ended, as it was his responsibility to ensure his scorecard was correct.

Daly went to Cape Cod to play in an exhibition pro-am match the next day. He rarely spoke to his amateur partners, he drove balls wherever he wanted on the course to amuse himself, and he hit his drives close to people playing in front of him. When Joe Concannon of the *Boston Globe* tried to question Daly about his disqualification in Hartford, he refused to acknowledge the reporter's presence.

It looked as if Daly's game might be coming back, however, after a flight across the North Atlantic. He was scheduled to play in two warm-up tournaments, the Irish and Scottish Opens, before playing in the British Open. His game was strong in Ireland, and Daly finished in second place.

After two previous appearances in the British Open, and several other European tournaments, Daly was as beloved by fans in the United Kingdom as he was in the United States. His Irish heritage had something to do with it, but the larger factor was the same as it was at home: fan identification. There were folks in the British Isles who were as fond of a smoke and a drink as Daly was, and there wasn't as much incessant worrying about the health effects of these activities as there was in the States. In many towns, a comfortable pub was the community center, where people of all ages gathered.

The average Brit also loved Daly for his refusal to renounce his working-class heritage. With upward social mobility much more difficult to manage in Britain than in the States, class consciousness was high. If people were going to be restrained in the lower classes, they were going to be damn proud of it— and not let anyone forget it. Even after Daly became a multimillionaire, he changed little about himself. That was why U.K. fans had cheered Daly's mammoth drives warmly as he was on his way to a last-place finish, and a tie for fourteenth, in the two previous British Opens. Daly explained it to the British press simply: "I am one of them."

It was this sense of familiarity, comfort, and acceptance— qualities that had often been missing in Daly's life—that led him into an interview with the British tabloid *The Sun* during his second week in Great Britain. After refusing to talk to journalists through the preliminaries of the Scottish Open, Daly talked to reporter Ben Bacon, who produced an article headlined "Dope Test All of Us." The subhead read: "It's the Only Way to Catch Stars Who Snort, Says Daly."

Saying he had been hurt when he went to rehab and people said he was the only PGA Tour player with a substance abuse problem, Daly declared: "I wish we could have drug testing on the tour. If we did, I'd probably be one of the cleanest guys out there.

"There are certain people on the tour who do the crazy stuff. They're never going to get exposed unless they are found out by the police and put in jail. Drugs, cocaine, some of the other crazy things. People said I was the crazy one on the tour, but others were getting up to much crazier things than me."

Daly said his alcoholism was still an everyday struggle, and he couldn't say he'd never drink again because the craving was always there. "I've been doing real well," he said, "even when I was in Ireland."

A sidebar to the main article was headlined "Daly Pleads: I Want to Help Golf's Drug Takers." The subhead was "John Daly Last Night Told Golf's Cocaine Takers: I'll Help You Beat Your Problem."

No one familiar with the tour or with Daly's record of antagonistic behavior could have taken his charges seriously. And given his extreme aversion to aftercare, even if there had been anyone else with a substance abuse problem, his offer to help was ludicrous. It was another case of John Daly flying off the rails. Few people in the media took the pieces as anything other than what they were—juicy, first-class British tabloid newspaper stories.

Such was not the case with Daly's compatriots on the PGA Tour. They had looked on for three years as Daly repeatedly and brazenly violated Deane Beman's most basic tenet: If you want to make a living in golf, conduct yourself like a faithful club pro and don't upset the sponsors. Daly had done everything in his power, short of turning to a life of crime, to upset the sponsors. And what had happened? The sponsors had given him a freaking $30 million contract, that's what had happened!

In the coming days, golfer Curtis Strange, acting as a spokesman for other members of the tour who appeared at a tournament he hosted, would tell the media: "What's really disturbing is that by making comments like this, John is capable of tearing down in a few minutes what Jack Nicklaus and Arnold Palmer have worked thirty-five years to build, and that's the image people have of the PGA Tour."

Implicit in Strange's words was a warning that the PGA Tour was going to collapse if somebody didn't do something about John Daly fast. As golf tournament directors around the globe could have told Strange, however, there wasn't another golfer they'd rather have in their events than John Daly. Far from being about to cause the demise of golf, John Daly had become the rainmaker of the sport. Everywhere he went with a driver in his hand, money leaked from the sky as joyful people danced around him with buckets.

Daly was indirectly demonstrating—however imperfectly and sometimes pathologically—that in the post–Deane Beman era, a golfer who had talent and worked to reach the fans didn't have to act like a club pro who had just been given clubhouse privileges. The golf market was changing, and the new fans wanted to connect with their favorite professional golfers, not look down on them. Rather than leading a revolution, Daly was reflecting changes that had already occurred. Most golf was now played on public-access courses, and to the minds of the people who patronized these layouts, Daly was symbolically wresting the game from the stranglehold of the twits.

When Daly came to the British Open, he talked to reporters briefly and began the long process of trying to square things with his fellow pros. "If I made some guys mad, I'm sorry. I'm not here to hurt anyone," he said, using a word he employed frequently when he was in trouble. Daly could be extraordinarily sensitive. He knew what it was like to have his feelings hurt, and he didn't want to do that to other people if he could help it. Then he went out to play a practice round, and as he was about to slug a drive off the tee, he said loudly enough for his gallery to hear: "Every time I look at the ball, I see my wife's face."

The requisite trip to the PGA Tour woodshed was awaiting Daly for his cocaine remarks, but this time the man with the switch in his hand wasn't Deane Beman. He had been replaced by his former deputy commissioner, Tim Finchem, in June. At forty-seven, Finchem was not a man who had come up through the ranks of golf. He was a lawyer who had worked for the Carter administration in the late 1970s before joining the tour's administrative staff in 1987.

Finchem met privately with Daly, then didn't hold a press conference, demonstrating that there were going to be some changes under the new administration. When reporters asked Finchem what had transpired at the meeting, he said it was tour policy not to disclose such information. The reporters responded that Beman had talked about Daly on a number of occasions, and Finchem fell back on his training in politics. The only reason Beman had spoken to the media then, Finchem said, was because "failure to do so would have created confusion."

With all the crap that was going down, and with his back still bothering him, Daly wasn't really into playing the exacting golf that was demanded by the links courses used for the British Open. Yet he still found himself sharing the lead after nine holes of the second round of the 1994 match at Turnberry Golf Links, in the Scottish town of the same name. Daly was using his length to advantage, but on the tenth hole the wildness that sometimes accompanies it did him in. He hooked his tee shot onto the beach at the seaside course, and even with a throng of fans helping, he wasn't able to find his ball and had to drop another.

On the eleventh hole he four-putted. After being five under par, he dropped to par in two holes. Since he was unlikely to win the tournament, Daly went through the motions for the final holes. He refused to talk to reporters, except to call back over his shoulder as he hurried to his car, "The whole day was disappointing. I'm just glad to survive. I'm going to go home and pull the knife out of my heart." Daly made the cut but finished last in the standings on Sunday.

Daly's back was bothering him so much when he returned to the States that he dropped out of the New England Classic in Sutton, Massachusetts, after the first round and had doctors perform a magnetic resonance imaging test. The results showed some enlarged and strained tissue but no real damage. Daly visited two more doctors while he was home for a tournament in Memphis. They also diagnosed it as inflammation and prescribed rest. But Daly was on another of his endurance runs, playing seven tournaments in a row, with more than a few paid outings mixed in. After having participated in three tournaments in Europe in July, he was headed back for more at the end of August.

Before he could go to Europe, Daly participated in the World Series of Golf, where he usually didn't play well. There were signs that Daly might be in one of his moods early in the week when Greg Norman, who was playing in front of Daly, had his caddie ask Daly to stop hitting his balls so close to Norman's group. On Saturday golfer Andrew Magee had an argument with Daly about the same topic after their round.

When he came to the fourteenth hole on Sunday, Daly was on his way to shooting an 83, which would put him fifteen over par for the tournament and well out of contention. The fourteenth hole was a dogleg, so the green wasn't visible from the tee. Daly's playing partner hit first with no problem, but Daly ripped one around the bend and the ball landed close to golfer Jeffrey Roth, who was on the green. Having a golf ball land nearby unexpectedly is always frightening, but in this case it seemed to be an accident and Roth didn't make an issue of it.

On the next hole, Roth was on the green getting ready to putt when Daly's ball came flying in like a miniature mortar shell and landed next to the green. This time it was a bigger deal. Roth was a club pro who had been invited to the World Series by virtue of his victory in a tournament with his peers. Being able to play a PGA Tour event was meaningful enough for Roth that he had brought his parents along with him. Having John Daly disrespect him this way, while his folks were standing there, magnified everything. Words were exchanged when Daly arrived at the fifteenth green.

Although Daly didn't hit close to them after that, there was still tension on the course over the last few holes. Roth finished the eighteenth hole and disappeared, and that seemed to be the end of it. But when Daly came out of the clubhouse after his round, Roth and his parents happened to be standing in the area. Roth muttered to Daly as he walked by. Daly could have kept going easily, yet there was something about this happy family unit standing there that forced him to respond. Daly stopped and got into Jeffrey Roth's face.

The two golfers sprayed words at each other. Tempers subsided after a moment, and Daly started to walk away. That was when Roth's father, Bob, felt compelled to call out: "Get a life, John." Daly turned and told the sixty-two-year-old man to get fucked.

Roth's mother, Dolores, had had quite enough of Daly's ill manners by this time. She told Daly that the entire affair had been his responsibility. He was the one who had started the unpleasantness by failing to practice proper golfing etiquette on the course.

The last time John Daly had heard this lecture was when he was sixteen years old. He and Chris Hentges and Brad

Struttmann were playing golf at the Jefferson City Country Club, and Daly drove a ball into the golf cart of the older women who were playing in front of them. He'd been forced to take a humiliating tongue-lashing then, because he was a kid and the women were mothers.

Now it was a similar situation, but with quite different dynamics. John Daly had become John Daly. Without missing a beat, Daly looked at Dolores Roth and told her to get fucked, too.

That was it for Bob Roth. Senior citizen or not, he wasn't going to stand there and have his lovely wife cursed at. As Daly turned to walk away, Roth—presumably without yelling "Yaaaaaaaaaaaahooooooooooooo"—made a running leap onto John Daly's back.

Three months after he had become golf's $30 million man, John Daly found himself lying on the ground outside the clubhouse of the Firestone Country Club, with a man who thought he was an attack dog attached to his back, while hundreds of spectators looked on, marveling at the extraordinary lengths Daly would go to in providing entertainment for his fans.

18

Truth in a Bottle

John Daly retreated to Memphis, while his people began talking intensively to reporters about how Daly was withdrawing from all golf obligations until he could find out how badly his painful back condition had been exacerbated by Bob Roth's piggyback ride. Comprehensive X-ray series were being scheduled in Memphis. Daly was sincerely sorry for disappointing all of his fans in Switzerland, where he was scheduled to appear next, but his medical situation dictated his indefinite absence from competition. Everyone was acutely concerned that this dire condition be fully remedied before Daly subjected his back to the rigors of tournament play. . . .

It was a superb effort, really, but it was subterfuge with no chance whatsoever of succeeding. International headlines about a club pro's father taking Daly to the deck in Akron, Ohio, like some tricked-up World Wrestling Federation pay-per-view special, meant another summit meeting at tour central. Yet again the question had to be raised: What on earth was going to be done about this magnificently talented and endlessly fallible young man?

September wasn't a good month for John Daly. He was so certain that his divorce from Bettye was finally going to come through that he had a celebration scheduled. He had to cancel the party when the dissolution of his marriage was pushed back yet again, this time until December.

After refusing to answer reporters' questions about what was to become of Daly in the aftermath of Akron, Tim Finchem reversed field and spoke at a press conference during a tournament on September 16. He said that Daly had volunteered to take the rest of the year off from golf and that his coming absence should not be considered a suspension.

"He does this with the hope of preparing himself mentally and physically to play on the tour," Finchem said. "We felt jointly he needed to take time out." The reporters all wrote that story, some putting the description of Daly's absence as being voluntary in quotation marks to signify that it was PR crap. Nobody believed it was anything less than a near suspension masquerading as a rest, except perhaps John Daly, whose talents for denial and self-delusion were exquisitely wrought.

John and Paulette were having a pleasant experience back home that weekend. After having rented a house for the better part of a year, they had moved into a new, custom-built $900,000 home in a golf-course development in suburban Memphis in late spring. They were still getting settled, but they took time out for a trip to Arkansas, where amid all the flaming arrows that were being fired at him of late, John was about to get an accolade. He was being inducted into the Razorback Hall of Honor at the University of Arkansas during ceremonies tied to the school's football game with the University of Alabama.

Arkansas gridiron teams weren't performing as they had in their days as a national football power, and that was leaving a lot of stadium seats uncovered during the bulk of the season. The university had expanded the capacity of its stadium in Fayetteville to 50,000 in 1985, only to have a succession of football squads have losing seasons in their conference. The day they enrolled John Daly and a handful of others associated with Arkansas athletics in the Hall of Honor, the university sold the place out for only the fourth time in nine years.

With the university making an effort to renew its ties with Daly, which only coincidentally came during another period when he was on hiatus from the tour, he had the opportunity to catch up with a former golf coach. Bill Woodley, the man who had tried to force Daly to confront his alcoholism seven years earlier only to have Daly flee from the university in response, still had his old job. As he watched Daly's career from afar, Woodley had often wondered how the early years of Daly's professional life might have been different if Woodley had been able to break through to Daly about his drinking. Woodley knew firsthand how thoroughly destructive alcoholism was, but he was also aware how little anyone other than the alcoholic can do about it.

With Daly stopping by the university, freshly chagrined and with time on his hands, Woodley decided to reach out to Daly again. He invited him to return to the school as a volunteer assistant golf coach for the fall. It was a way to try to bring one of the institution's most famous and prosperous dropouts back into the Razorback fold, and it would blow away the kids on the golf team. John Daly had worn out squadrons of people who had tried to help him with his life in the past decade. Ultimately, Daly's recalcitrance had caused most of them to shrug in resignation. When someone he hadn't burnt out yet offered friendship, Daly accepted it eagerly.

While he was being welcomed back by his university, Daly was being treated more curtly by his sponsors. Reebok announced in late September that it was suspending Daly's endorsement contract until he returned to the tour in January. The company said Daly needed to "get his act back together," because "he's not marketable while he's not playing."

At a time when everyone was hoping that Daly was finally going to change, he seemed most interested—as always—in denying that his actions of recent months, like so many other negatives in his life, had anything to do with his alcoholism. In a prepared statement accompanying Reebok's announcement, Daly was quoted as saying, "I am working with them to put together a comprehensive physical training program which should help in my return."

A few days later, Wilson Sporting Goods announced that it also was pulling Daly's contract while he was away from the tour. The company said they would resume their relationship "under a newly restructured agreement" when it was satisfied Daly had met specific behavioral and performance objectives.

Daly's accompanying statement talked about golfing skills and physical conditioning first, and only mentioned in passing that there was a problem with his behavior. "I plan to practice and prepare myself as much as possible so that when I return to professional competition, I will play and conduct myself at the level Wilson and my fans have come to expect."

Daly accompanied the University of Arkansas golf team to the Jerry Pate National Intercollegiate Tournament at Shoal Creek Golf Club, in Birmingham, Alabama, at the end of October. Even though he was twenty-eight now, Daly hadn't forgotten what it was like to be a college kid. There were teams from twelve schools competing in the event, and as usual, they had a boring dinner planned at which all the players would have to eat bad food and listen to insipid speakers while holding to their best behavior. Daly knew what a drag that was, so shortly after the dinner began, he sneaked the boys from the Razorback golf team out of the dining room and took them on a field trip to a strip club in town.

There were reporters from the Associated Press and the *Atlanta Journal-Constitution* at the tournament, and they asked Daly how he was handling his voluntary suspension. Daly asked them whatever in the world they were talking about. "That was all my doing," he said, fully aware that what he was saying was going to appear in newspapers across the country. "I didn't give Tim the chance to sit me down. I told him I wasn't going to play the rest of the year because of my back. It was just a voluntary withdrawal. I needed some time off, and I said it's not fair to the tour for me to go overseas and play when I'm not playing the regular tour."

Daly claimed that Finchem had said this was a fine idea. In fact, Daly said, Finchem had commended him for making such a smart decision—and all of his own accord, too.

Daly said he understood how the reporters could have gotten such a false impression, as he was frequently the target of unfair media coverage, which resulted in people having these distorted images of him. Take, for example, his remarks about drug use on the tour. That had all been taken out of context. Daly hadn't meant to hurt anyone, and Daly himself had been hurt when the other players reacted so badly to the story.

Then there was the World Series affair. He had apologized for hitting into Jeffrey Roth, and everything that happened after that was Daly trying to defend himself against the harassment of the Roth family. He told Glenn Sheeley from the Atlanta paper, "Where does a player stand out where he can't defend himself? I think that's what hurts the most. I have often thought, what if it had been someone else that had hit into him?"

Ultimately, Daly told the reporters, it always came down to the same universal truth. He was just a country boy, and everybody in the world knew that it took country boys a little longer to learn things than most people. "I wasn't born with a silver spoon in my mouth," he said, "with somebody to teach me right from wrong."

Along those lines, he said that he really didn't understand why Reebok and Wilson had suspended his contracts, but that they pretty much had to do what they had to do, for whatever reason they wanted.

About preparing to return to the tour, Daly said that was just a matter of his getting in shape, getting the old back tightened up, then he'd be out there ready to go again, just like old times.

As long as people continued to tolerate Daly's behavior, or enable it, as they say in recovery circles, things would go on like old times. Daly would be returning to Australia early in 1995 to play in the Heineken Classic, the Skins Game, and the Australian Masters—the last tournament being one Daly had gotten himself disqualified from in 1992 for a scorecard violation, before blowing town with his $35,000 appearance fee. Having been burned that way once, organizers of the Australian events weren't going to risk that kind of money again. Instead, they were going to pay Daly ten times as much—$375,000—to play in three golf tournaments, all the while praying to God on bended knee that Daly didn't throw a fit of rage before enough people had rushed through the gates for them to turn a profit.

But there were other people in John Daly's life who were realizing something monumental. There were questions about Daly and his behavior that had never been answered definitively and objectively. When Daly left the tour in September 1994, reporters had asked PGA Tour commissioner Tim Finchem if he thought Daly's behavior at the British Open and at Akron was alcohol-related. Finchem said, "There is no indication we have arising out of any incidents that relates to his situation that indicates any substance abuse whatsoever."

But the commissioner had an important proviso: "Having said that, we want to explore whatever kinds of assistance we can offer to his preparation as a player. We will continue to have discussions about the specifics of that."

Because the control alcohol has over alcoholics is absolute, and the possibilities of relapse once an addict gets sober are measureless, many rehabilitation programs—including those mandated for physicians who are alcoholics—require that recovering alcoholics be tested regularly for any traces of intoxicants in their systems. It is a gentle but pointed way to remind alcoholics that their days of deceiving people—and themselves—about their drinking are irrevocably over.

With such testing confronting them, many sober alcoholics are able to refrain from taking that first drink because they know they will be caught if they do. John Daly, through his many suspensions and absences from golf, and with a drinking history that included Herculean binges—he had sometimes rolled kegs of beer into his hotel room to slake his thirst—and multiple hospitalizations, had never been obliged to meet this criteria.

When Daly spoke to reporters in Mexico City after his suspension in November 1993 at the Kapalua Bay tournament in Hawaii, he said that if anybody thought he was still drinking, he would be happy to get tested to prove he wasn't. No one asked him to get tested. Eight months later, at the 1994 British Open, Daly provoked outrage with his remarks about cocaine, but his underlying message then had been the same: Test golfers for substance abuse. John Daly was a man with drug testing so much on his mind that he kept getting reporters to write about it in connection with his name. Someone finally picked up on this.

Although it wouldn't be announced, John Daly would begin submitting to monthly substance abuse tests when he returned to the tour in 1995. The results would be sent to the tour office by the laboratory. Daly's compliance with this program was, of course, entirely voluntary.

19

Outliving the Past

Not much was heard of John Daly from the middle of November until he returned to action at the first tournament of 1995 in Carlsbad, California, in early January. There had been several significant changes in his life since the last time he had played golf professionally, at the World Series. Bettye, finally and officially, had become his ex-wife. He had been granted regular visitation with Shynah, who would be delivered to her father by her nanny, thereby avoiding any uncomfortable encounters between the little girl's parents. Shynah wouldn't be lacking for a playmate when she visited—in a few years, anyway—for Paulette Dean was now four months pregnant. On Wednesday she and John ducked out of the LaCosta resort, where the tournament was being held, and kept a doctor's appointment. They discovered they were going to have a daughter.

John and Paulette shared their happy news with reporters at the tournament, and John spoke of his feelings for the woman he had met at a golf tournament only a couple of hours drive away. "Paulette is a super girl," he said. "She makes me happy and is so good for me. I believe she is the girl I will share my life with. For someone just twenty-three, she is amazingly mature."

John said he was returning to the tour with a renewed drive to win, but he still seemed to be searching for an explanation for the mess that his life sometimes became. "Though my parents brought me up very strict," he said, "I lived in a country town. You don't know what's going on in the rest of the world until you get out there. I had to make a lot of decisions that I wasn't prepared to make."

Daly hadn't played competitive golf in over four months, and he came to the tournament with surprisingly sensible expectations: He didn't want to finish last. Daly started slow, with a 75, but his scores dropped every day until his final round of 69, giving him a tie for twentieth place in the field of thirty-one. It was a good start, but already his impatience was showing. He started talking about being in contention by Phoenix, which was only three weeks away.

He finished last in Hawaii the following week, then missed the cut at both Tucson and Phoenix during the final weeks of January. When he and Paulette found themselves otherwise unoccupied that weekend in Phoenix, and with Las Vegas only three hundred miles away, they decided, what the hell, let's get married. John was a highly social man. He preferred to have people around him most of the time, and even with his constant travels, he maintained an extensive network of friendships outside of professional golf, where he was close only to Fuzzy Zoeller. But since his big blowout wedding in Blytheville with Dale, John had developed a preference for more intimate ceremonies in his subsequent marriages.

John and Paulette had the Las Vegas wedding that Bettye, in order not to commit bigamy, had denied John. They went to the Little Church of the West for the ceremony. John's former caddie had gotten married there, and he spoke highly of their service. John wore jeans, cowboy boots, and a dark coat with no tie. Paulette, who was getting married for the first time, wore a white mini-suit and carried a bouquet of peach roses that John bought for her. The ceremony lasted fifteen minutes, whereupon Paulette Dean became the third Mrs. John Daly.

There wasn't much time to celebrate or gamble in Vegas, as John and Paulette were flying to Australia on Sunday night, where they would have a working honeymoon that criss-crossed the Australian continent. John's first tournament was in Perth, at the extreme western edge of the country.

Making prolonged flights, such as the journey from the western perimeter of the United States to the far end of Australia, was extremely stressful for John, and it was one of the times when he missed the narcotic effects of alcohol the most. The temptations weren't going to abate in Perth, either, as the golf tournament was being sponsored by Heineken beer. The company's familiar green advertising signs would be abundant at the event, as would thousands of people who were cheerfully, sometimes boisterously, consuming the brewer's products. Daly's memories of the gorgeous taste of a frigid beer after a long afternoon in the baking sun on a golf course would be all too familiar. Substance abuse tests were created for situations like this.

Even though he was coming off a last-place finish and two missed cuts, Daly was heading for Australia with determination. His New Year's resolution had been to forget the past, but he was anxious to show Australian golf fans that this was a new John Daly who was paying them a return visit—one who no longer walked away when his game wasn't perfect. Rededicated after his latest four-month absence from his profession, Daly was going to behave himself, he was going to charm his galleries as only he could, and—given the humongous appearance fees he was earning—he was going to insure that he made the cut in the events that had one.

Daly had concluded that, as every authority in the world of golf had been telling him for years, he had to tame his game down if he wanted to win more frequently. He had done it in Atlanta in 1994 and won, and now he had decided to play that way all the time. He was going to move toward the norm on the PGA Tour and become more of a cautious, high-percentage player.

"I want to be here for the four days and not just two," Daly told reporters when he arrived in Perth. "I think the fans understand that. The name of the game is trying to win tournaments. When I didn't try my best, I disappointed a lot of people who wanted to see me in contention." Therefore, Daly said, he would be hitting a ton of two-irons off the tee, with only the occasional driver thrown in.

For weeks there had been tremendous expectations about Long John Daly, the Wild Thing, coming to Perth to work his particular miracle with golf balls. With all the hype that had preceded him, and with Perth being as isolated as it was, this seemed like a once-in-a-lifetime opportunity for many local golfers. They were going to be able to see John Daly, the Yank golf-ball assassin, in person. The mythical stories about how far he had once hit the ball in a windstorm or on an aircraft carrier deck were rampant. To the locals, this was really a bit of golf history they were going to be seeing here.

Then the all-powerful legend appears and says he wants to hit two-iron? What kind of rot was this? It was like going to one of the nudie bars that Daly had patronized on occasion and hearing the girls say they had a bit of a chill, so they wouldn't be taking their tops off that night. Wasn't it nearly criminal, taking a $125,000 per-tournament appearance fee and then hitting two-iron?

Perth was a town of considerable wealth, dotted with skyscrapers in which accountants tallied the money corporations earned extracting interminable shiploads of minerals and oil from the surrounding land. The relatively small population of Perth paid such a disproportionate share of the country's taxes that there was a movement afoot to secede from Australia. And John Daly thought he was going to get away with hitting two-iron in a town like this? "If he doesn't pull out the driver," Heineken Classic tournament director Tony Roosefburg told reporters, "he's liable to have a riot on his hands."

Using his two-iron most of the time, Daly shot 80 during the first round of the tournament, putting him fourteen strokes off the lead and in danger of missing the cut. Of the eight bogeys he had in the round, seven had come when he hit iron off the tee. Quickly enough Daly decided he had made a mistake, declaring his change of heart to the impatient spectators. "I think I was put on this earth to use a driver," he said.

Two weeks later Daly's resolve was back, as he used his driver only twice on a tight, tree-lined course during the first round of the Australian Masters and shot a two under. He loosened up a bit on Friday and hit the driver six times, while still shooting 69 and impressing the locals with his terrific short game rather than only with his length. He was also publicly contrite about his bad behavior three years earlier, attributing it to his drinking during that visit. Like its counterpart in the States, the Australian Masters positions itself as a historic tournament, and all of this went over well with the galleries there. Daly didn't win the Heineken Classic or the Australian Masters, but using two different approaches, he left the country with many more fans than he had arrived with.

When it was time for the American Masters Tournament in April, the Daly motor home rolled into Augusta, Georgia, as if it were a homecoming weekend. Ray Hentges, Daly's coach from Helias High School, was there early in the week. A friend of Hentges from Jefferson City had practice-round tickets, which were no longer freely available, and Hentges had come down with Jim Rackers, the Helias principal. Hentges had joked to Rackers that they might be able to stay for the tournament, because Hentges intended to hit Daly up for tickets once he saw him at the golf course. They both had a good laugh over that, as they were certain Daly had distributed his tickets months earlier. Then Daly said sure, he had two tickets. He had secured them for his parents, and they weren't coming. Never anticipating this could happen, Rackers had made other plans, and so he and Hentges couldn't use the tickets, either.

Bill Woodley was down from the University of Arkansas for the week as John's guest. He was helping him work on his game and providing moral support. Trying to teach Daly anything was always tricky. You had to make it sound as though you were pointing out something he might want to think about, and it had to sound spontaneous, like: "Hey, I just had this wild idea, why don't you try this?" The way it worked was, first you had to see what he was doing wrong, then you had to figure out how you could tell him about it to make it sound as though he weren't doing anything wrong but maybe could do it better. Mostly they worked on his putting, because that was critical at Augusta.

Daly finished tied for forty-fifth, which wasn't terrific, but he could deal with it. He had brought this amazing and uncharacteristic mellowness back from his fall absence from the tour, which even his friends didn't recognize. He wasn't scoring stunning numbers on the course, and he wasn't even remotely in contention, but it felt okay. Daly could almost intuit good things in the making. He was just waiting for them to manifest themselves in his game. "It feels close," he was telling reporters. "I don't know if it's a win, but it's not far from being there."

He was confident enough about this that he played at Hilton Head, in the South Carolina coastal lowlands, the week after the Masters. This was not a John Daly course. The fairways on the Pete Dye–designed layout were as narrow as a model's waist, and they were overhung by enough densely foliated trees to start an arboretum. Without the tournament galleries to help him look, this was a course on which John Daly in the wild mode could lose as many balls in a round as the average weekend golfer.

Daly didn't make the mistake of announcing that he was going to play conservatively there, as he had in Perth, and no one paid that much attention when he went ahead and did it anyway. He finished tied for thirteenth—his best performance of the year—while quietly cranking up his self-confidence another notch, even as his driving-distance average was decreasing by two yards.

He missed the cut in Houston, then came back to the Bell-South Classic outside Atlanta, having all those good memories from the previous year's win. He shot a solid 67 the first day, but he was in a bit of a funk. For the second consecutive year, he was in early contention in this tournament, in a town where the fans lionized him. What could the problem be? Daly puzzled over it, and when he couldn't figure out anything else, he decided it must be his hair, which was now grown in and looked pretty much like everybody else's hair.

Daly consulted with his hair stylist du jour, Darren Norwood, a local country-and-western singer, who was visiting with John during the tournament. John was trying to teach himself the guitar, and he was getting free lessons from people everywhere he went. John plopped down in front of Darren and told him to do something inspired with his hair. Darren begot a hairdo that resembled a smashed-down French Foreign Legionnaire's hat: short and flat on the top, but long and flowing at the neck, the better to keep the desert sand from blowing inside one's shirt.

The haircut's charm worked for a day, as John shot another 67 on Friday to claim a one-stroke lead in the tournament. "The spectators were pretty rowdy most of the day," he said afterward. "I can't wait until tomorrow. I hope it gets loud." It was noisy initially, but Daly's touch went cold and he dropped to a tie for twelfth place by the time all the shouting was over on Sunday.

Daly missed another Friday cut at the end of May in Fort Worth, Texas, and he blew out of there in search of distraction from the pressure of playing badly. By Saturday evening he was in Tunica, Mississippi, steeping himself in the melodic tones being emitted by the slot machines at the Horseshoe Casino. The Horseshoe was one of a number of gambling halls located across the state border from Memphis, down that famous Highway 61 that Bob Dylan had sung about.

Since Daly was a man whose sensibilities weren't attuned to moderation, he was inclined to keep things interesting when he gambled. At twenty-nine he had already accumulated more than enough wealth to last him for the rest of this life—and there were additional funds arriving weekly. With that kind of capital, an experienced gambler had to put a hefty sum into play to drive his pulse up a point or two. When Daly decided to absent himself from the table games and play the slots that evening at the Horseshoe, he headed for the Red, White & Blue machines and selected a one-armed bandit that required $100 tokens. On one exceptionally unlikely spin of the reels, lights began flashing and even more bells began to ring, and a crowd gathered. On his Saturday night off from golf, Daly had won a $100,000 slot machine jackpot.

When the smiling manager came out with an oversized check, followed by an assistant with a camera, Daly knew exactly what to do. He employed his golf tournament technique: He held the check up in front of his chest and gave the photographer a little halfhearted grin. Before Daly left the casino, the manager had him sign some forms, which Daly didn't think much about.

Back home after his good fortune, Daly had more momentous matters to attend to. On Thursday Paulette was expected to give birth to their daughter, whom they were naming Sierra—which also happened to be the name of the rehab center John had attended. The impending birth of his second child was accompanied by John's experiencing some unusual physical discomfort. After years of drinking phenomenal amounts of alcohol and seldom having a hangover, Daly had suddenly begun having severe headaches, which were lasting up to ten hours.

With his childhood having been so itinerant, Daly was still having trouble planting roots as an adult. He had enjoyed his work with the University of Arkansas golf team enough that he decided he should move his family up to Rogers, Arkansas, outside of Fayetteville, so he could practice there and continue his work with the team. He put his Memphis house on the market, having lived there a little over a year.

With all the confusion in his personal life, Daly was playing lousy golf, missing the cut at the U.S. Open and at the Hartford tournament the following week. His headaches were worse than ever on Friday in Hartford, and he was due to play in the St. Jude tournament in Memphis the following week. Daly had played in Memphis the previous year with a bad back, but he decided that even though his house overlooked the course where the event was being staged, and people were going to be upset, he was going to bag it this year. He notified a PGA Tour representative on Friday that he was withdrawing from St. Jude.

On Saturday morning the Memphis *Commercial Appeal* ran a story on the first page of the sports section with a headline saying that tournament officials were shocked to learn of Daly's withdrawal. The piece went on to say that Daly hadn't given a reason for dropping out of the tournament, but that he had missed the cut in Hartford. For local people familiar with Daly's history, this was an opportunity to think the worst: Daly was flipping out again.

Then their Sunday papers arrived, and right in the first section was a big ad for the Horseshoe Casino lauding the looseness of their slot machines and the largess of their jackpots. Prominently featured at the top of the ad was a photo of John Daly holding his oversized $100,000 check. Although Memphis has an active and funky music scene and lively nightlife, the state of Tennessee is still known as the buckle of the Bible belt. By Sunday afternoon there were a fair number of folks around Memphis who thought that John Daly's splitting from the St. Jude had something to do, one way or the other, with the wages of sin.

Even with his headaches, Daly found it impossible to pass up a paid outing on Cape Cod on the Monday of St. Jude week, partly because, as in Australia, he had some amends to make there as well. He had behaved badly during his one-day visit to the pro-am tournament in 1994. This year he was generous with his time and attention with the participants, the spectators, and even the media. He gave reporters the same message he had been repeating since the beginning of the year: He was playing steady golf, and even though he wasn't winning, that was okay, because he knew he was close.

Daly returned to Memphis after the match, where Paulette and Sierra were waiting for him, and so were the people who ran the St. Jude. He was going to have to fix that, plus do some damage control on the rumors that had been flying around town about his gambling since the casino advertisement ran. When Daly had gambled in South Africa and Las Vegas, reports of his activities seldom reached home. That changed when he gave the Horseshoe permission to use his photo in their advertising.

Daly decided to handle the rumors by giving an interview to Bobby Hall, the golf writer for the Memphis paper. Daly invited Hall into his home office, where the decorations include a stuffed adult hog, the team mascot of the Arkansas Razorbacks. Hall asked Daly if he had been doing some gambling down in Mississippi, and Daly said that he had. "Yeah, I gamble," he said. "I gamble for fun and pleasure. I do it because I can, and it's relaxing. It's the most relaxing thing I do besides playing the guitar."

When Daly had given up hard liquor for beer, and people tried to get him to leave beer alone, he would say: "I am not going to quit drinking beer." When he finally gave up beer but kept smoking as many as three or four packs of cigarettes a day, and people got on him, he said: "I am not going to quit smoking cigarettes." Anticipating the remarks—which Daly took as criticism—the casino ad was going to provoke, Daly tried to pinch them off before they were voiced. If people had learned anything about John Daly by now, it should at least be the guiding principle of his life: No one was going to tell him what to do.

Daly told Hall that he didn't think there was anything wrong with going to a casino for a two- to three-hour visit, but that given his personality, he had trouble holding it to that. He said he loved gambling so much that he was spending twelve to twenty-four hours at a stretch in casinos. But, he said with his characteristic conviction, "I'm not going to quit gambling."

Dough Boy II

John Daly consulted with doctors about his headaches, and when they found nothing amiss, he slipped out of Memphis en route to Rogers, Arkansas, to do some business and to work on his game. Daly's people had been negotiating with another potential sponsor, Hudson Foods, a poultry company that was based in Rogers. The company's chairman, Red Hudson, liked to use professional golfers for business entertaining, and he was about to sign Daly to a three-year deal.

John and Paulette had been planning to do some intensive house hunting in Rogers during this time, but the real-estate market for near-million-dollar homes in Memphis was proving to be dormant. John liked to move whenever the impulse struck him, but he kept forgetting that only one of his houses had wheels. His dwellings were getting more extravagant with each relocation, and this was becoming an expensive indulgence. Realtors told the Dalys that they could lose $250,000 if they insisted on selling their Memphis house after such a short time in residence. They took that house off the market—then made an offer on a place in Rogers anyway.

John didn't have another tournament scheduled until the middle of July, when he would be playing in the British Open, the year's third major. He was planning to do something uncommon in his professional career—he was going to spend three weeks getting ready for one tournament. Part of his motivation was his headaches. His doctors had told him to rest, and he figured practicing was more restful than being in competition.

But a more important factor was the new perspective he had on his career. He was beginning to accept that he wasn't going to win many tournaments by sheer bombast alone, and that if he wanted to win more often—and he did—he was going to have to polish the rest of his game. Hiding out in Rogers, hitting golf balls with the fortitude he used to save for drinking, was part of his program to become a more complete golfer.

His golf bag was a work in progress, as Wilson Sporting Goods kept shipping him prototypes of new high-tech clubs and balls. Daly was working with the company to develop the products that CEO John Riccitiello planned to use to turn their golf division around. Daly particularly liked a new driver they had created. It produced a lower ball flight while seeming to offer more control. This would be beneficial at the British Open, as the winds at the coastal courses that hosted the tournament could be fierce.

This year's Open was being staged at the Old Course at St. Andrews, Scotland, the most celebrated venue in golf. It was the oldest golf course in the world, with a history dating to the shepherds who originated the game. A British Open was played there for the first time in 1873. John Daly had competed in the Dunhill Cup at St. Andrews in 1993, and he had won four of his five matches.

Just as diligently as he was working on his game, Daly was striving to smooth his relations with the other players on the tour. There still weren't a lot of golfers inviting John and

Paulette out for dinner—and vice versa—but rather than walking into the locker room with anger in his eyes, Daly was making an effort to diminish the resentment with small gestures. He didn't expect most of the other golfers to become his confidants, but he wanted to cool off some of the close-to-the-surface hostility. Daly decided the best way for him to make amends was to continue with his best behavior, as he had been doing since January.

When he had refused to attend aftercare upon leaving rehabilitation in 1993, Daly had evidenced what addiction counselors call "self-will run riot," or the belief that he could resist alcohol on his own. Until alcoholics abandon this posture, some counselors say they aren't in recovery—that healing requires complete humility and submission to higher authority. This is manifested most saliently at AA meetings, in which alcoholics publicly confess to the ills liquor has caused them.

Daly had resisted AA because of this very feature, saying he could never play golf the next day after hearing such depressing stories. Yet when he returned to golf in January 1995, he suddenly began exhibiting AA-type behavior toward the tour. Whenever his past troubles were raised, Daly said they had been solely his fault, and whenever there was a question about an action by the tour's administration, Daly's comment was that whatever they had done was correct. Daly's copping this attitude must have had Deane Beman thinking comeback.

Not everyone on the tour thought that Daly should be exchanging his old wardrobe for one tailored from sackcloth decorated with Reebok and Wilson logos. His allies included David Feherty, an Irishman who had become friends with Daly when they were playing the Sunshine Tour together in South Africa in 1990. Feherty had set a course record of 62 during the first round of the AECI Charity Classic at Rand

Park in Johannesburg, in February of that year, and he seemed well on his way to a blowout over the rest of the tournament field.

Daly was eight shots behind Feherty after the first round, five shots after the second. During the third round Daly matched Feherty's two-day-old course record of 62 and pulled within one shot of him. All day, each day, Feherty kept looking at the leaderboard, and back over his shoulder, thinking to himself, in Butch Cassidy fashion: "Who is this guy and why won't he go away?"

Feherty rallied and recovered a four-stroke lead after nine holes of the final round, only to hook a ball into a water hazard on the fourteenth hole. Meanwhile Daly never stumbled. He came to the final green needing to make a twelve-foot birdie to win, and he slid it into the side of the cup.

Feherty was taken with the sheer indomitability and fearlessness of this twenty-three-year-old Yank, who was operating in South Africa at the moment, but who was clearly prepared to take on the world. Feherty recognized in Daly a constitution he admired—made all the more winning by Daly's naïveté—and regardless of the outcome of the tournament, the two men became friends.

Feherty came to the States from Europe in 1994 and began playing on the American tour. He didn't make a lot of headlines, but he quietly went about his business. As Daly was involved in one uproar after another, Feherty looked on, thinking that a lot of it was being blown out of proportion and that even more of it was being driven by resentment of Daly's ability to flaunt Uncle Deane's rules and still get rich.

Finally, just as—unbeknownst to Feherty—Daly was trying to lead a low-profile life for the first time ever, Feherty, who was going through a divorce, decided he had had enough of the locker-room sniping by men who, he believed, wouldn't have survived half of Daly's struggles. When reporters asked

Feherty on Tuesday of British Open week about Daly's past notoriety, Feherty unloaded.

"Players don't like him, and it's professional jealousy," Feherty said. "A lot of them would like to see him out of golf. Why? Because he behaves the way he does and gets away with it, and because he's got a $30 million contract. That's the way he is, but good luck to him. John Daly is the best thing to happen to golf since Arnold Palmer showed up. He doesn't drink anymore, and he's dried out, yet he is still only in his late twenties. With the failed marriage and all the crap that's heaped on him for all and sundry, he still comes back and wins a bit of money, wins tournaments, and delights the crowds."

Allowing that Daly "wasn't very sensible at times," Feherty talked about how Daly invigorated the galleries at golf tournaments in a way that was extremely beneficial to the sport. These matters had been overlooked in Daly's string of troubles, and Feherty didn't want his fellow pros to forget about them. Then he issued a warning of sorts. "If ever there were a golf course built to suit John Daly," he said, "this is it."

There weren't many people in golf who agreed with Feherty on his final point. Given his poor performance in past British Opens and his bleak play on the regular tour during the first half of 1995, no one thought Daly was going to be anything more than a novelty item at the British Open Championship—and one with a two-day shelf life at that. In licensed British betting shops, wagers on Daly's winning were being accepted at sixty-six to one. The oddsmaker for *USA Today* found the whole notion so preposterous that he had Daly listed at five hundred to one.

When reporters asked Daly to respond to Feherty's remarks, Daly evaded their questions, except those about him winning. "This is a course I love more than any other, because it is so much fun," he said. "I'll hit a lot of drivers this week, but I'm putting less pressure on myself to win, and enjoying my golf much more as a result. I'm not forcing things any longer."

Among the things Daly wasn't forcing were questions of whether the tour had the right to ordain his behavior. Although Daly had to be heartened by Feherty's defense, he was essentially saying, "Look, I don't want any trouble here." After three marriages, two children, and five years in the big leagues of golf, John Daly was sounding perilously close to being grown-up.

That maturity showed on the course on Thursday, when Daly focused on being patient—not getting aggravated when play was slow, not racing to his ball, and not hurrying his swing. He was more under control than he had ever been in a major. Yet the wide fairways at St. Andrews allowed him to slug his driver on the majority of holes. The combination of these two factors put Daly in a four-way tie for first place at the end of one round, with a score of 67.

Daly told reporters that if he could keep the ball straight, he could do well in the tournament. Right there he was putting pressure on himself by giving voice to his expectations. That wasn't part of the syllabus for the all-new, totally controlled, and repentant John Daly persona. But as Daly himself liked to say, you can't take everything away from a person's past.

Daly remembered that slogan on Friday. On the fifth hole he put his drive in one of the bunkers that punctuate the Old Course with the same frequency that craters adorn a minefield after an invasion. Pot bunkers that are the depth and diameter of manholes pervade the course, and most of them are invisible from the tee. Others bunkers have the dimensions of small in-ground backyard swimming pools. So fearsome are these sand holes, that like the Hell Bunker and the Principal's Nose, they have names.

The first time Daly attempted to extricate his ball from a

bunker on the fifth hole, it stayed in. The second time he resigned himself to hitting out sideways and thus not advancing his ball. When he finally holed out, he had lost two strokes to par. Since the hole was a par five, and one that Daly would be expected to birdie, it was the equivalent of dropping three shots.

Playing in a distant land, and without alcohol to steel his nerves, Daly's only comfort on the course was to block out thoughts of what had just occurred. He had to stay focused narrowly and exclusively ahead, letting nothing from the past enter his consciousness. Then he reached the eighth hole. There was a vendor near the tee there who was selling chocolate doughnuts. These weren't the elixir food of Jefferson City—refrigerator biscuits with chocolate gravy—but, my God, this was a golf course in Scotland in the midst of the British Open, and with them having the two essential ingredients, chocolate and dough, they were pretty damn close!

Daly savaged four of them, right there on the tee, as thousands looked on at the odd sight, their jackets fastened tight around their necks against the biting afternoon wind off the sea. The spectators didn't realize they were witnessing food as magic—that Daly was soothing himself with digestible comfort. Chris Hentges and Brad Struttmann hadn't understood, either, back when they were all sixteen and John breakfasted on platters of chocolate-covered biscuits that made him invincible.

The Scottish doughnuts were wonderful and strong, and their impact was amplified when Daly administered himself a chocolate-chip muffin as a booster shot on the 10th tee. Soon the bunker from the fifth hole receded into his memory, and Daly played his way into the clubhouse with a round of 71 that put him at six under par. At the halfway point of the oldest major golf tournament in the world, John Daly, the five-hundred-to-one shot out of Dardanelle, Arkansas, was tied for the lead.

As soon as Daly came into the media center for his interview, the reporters started kidding him about pigging out on the course. Back in Jefferson City, his eating habits, and the physique they produced, had been a source of embarrassment for Daly. He would cringe in silent pain, or have another beer, every time someone brought them up—however innocuously.

Yet sitting in the pressroom, among people he usually considered the enemy, John Daly had an epiphany. He suddenly realized that despite what he kept hearing, he had another option available besides fleeing from his past. He could accept it—in its totality—as being a huge chunk of the only life he was ever going to have. And he could learn from it. Then he could go on.

Daly told the reporters how much he had enjoyed the pastries he ate on the course, then paused for a moment. "You know," he said, out of the blue, "my nickname can be Dough Boy. They called me Dough Boy in high school. Now I don't mind if they call me Dough Boy out here."

Someone said that Daly was going to get really fat if he kept eating doughnuts like that. "Listen," he said, "as long as my pants fit, I really don't care."

A reporter asked Daly how he felt about holding a share of the lead at the midpoint of the tournament. "Hell, I'm amazed," he said. "I think a lot of people are. If I can keep patient, I've got a chance. I just hope that if I stay in contention, the galleries will get rowdy out there. I love that."

The Road Home

The spectators in Scotland, billed as the world's most discerning golf galleries, were as appreciative as those in the United States when John Daly hit a flock of killer drives on Saturday. Even with the expectation in the United Kingdom that public behavior will be restrained, the extravagance of Daly's shots bounding down the rock-hard fairways at St. Andrews forced otherwise reserved people to exclaim loudly.

Daly's distance off the tee, however, didn't translate into birdies on Saturday. The wind was up again, and wildness crept into his game. On the eighteenth hole he slipped while hitting a giant drive that carried beyond the green, which was 354 yards away. He was saved when his ball ricocheted off an obstruction and back into play.

The numbers on Saturday weren't encouraging. An unfamiliar young player, Michael Campbell from New Zealand, shot a 65, while Daly was one over at 73. Daly's two-day stint atop the leaderboard was finished, and he was four shots off the pace. Having Campbell charge by him seemed to take the fight out of Daly, and he sank into his recently wrought cautious mode. He told reporters that he hoped he could catch the New Zealander, but he said, "The Old Course is not a course you can really attack. You have to be careful."

Asked if, given his experience at the PGA, Daly had any advice for the novice who was leading the tournament, Daly could only joke weakly, "I'd say just go out and make three or four double bogeys."

Daly was unsettled that night, and he and Paulette didn't get to sleep until 3:30 A.M. Even when his most severe bouts of drinking sent him to bed with near-inflammable breath, John was always a morning man. Sun's up: out of bed, feet on the deck, into action. When Daly climbed out of bed early on Sunday morning, he heard the winds howling off the sea at forty miles per hour, foretelling a strenuous day on the links.

Fortunately, the pantry at his hotel was well stocked with chocolate-covered dough—with a French accent, no less. After bolstering himself with a half-dozen chocolate croissants, with eggs on the side, Daly turned his attention to the care of his spirits. His tee time wasn't until after two o'clock that afternoon, so he watched *Mr. Baseball* and *Another Stakeout* in the room, then cranked up some jams on a stereo. While other golfers were flailing at balls on the practice range, John Daly was dancing madly with his wife to rock and roll.

Over at the Old Course, Jack Nicklaus was playing his final round of the tournament, en route to finishing seventy-ninth. Nicklaus had racked up an astounding ten strokes on the four-teenth hole on Thursday, after hitting into the Hell Bunker and taking four strokes to get out. He'd finished with a 78 but came back with a 70 on Friday to barely stay under the cut line of 149. No one had expected him to be a front-runner in the competition, but then again, there weren't many fifty-five-year-old men who even made it into the field.

Between 1964 and 1979 Nicklaus had won three British

Opens and been the runner-up seven times, compiling one of the most splendid records in the tournament's fabled history. Those days were memories now. Although as a former champion he had ten years of tournament eligibility left, Nicklaus announced at the 1995 Open that he would be participating in future British Opens only on an irregular basis.

Nicklaus had also been a part-time ABC commentator at the tournament in recent years, putting on the earphones after his round when time allowed. Since he would be playing in only a few more Opens, his days of contributing to its broadcast were also probably ending. With his income from endorsements alone estimated at over $14 million a year, Nicklaus didn't need to fly his jet over to the U.K. to pick up ice cream money working for TV.

So when Jack Nicklaus walked into the broadcast booth on July 23, 1995, there were trolleyloads of baggage clanging along behind him, much of it draped with championship ribbons that were fading. Among the first questions his announcing colleagues asked Nicklaus, after he got settled, was how he liked Daly's chances that afternoon.

"I don't think this is his day," Nicklaus said. "Daly will have a tough time in this wind because, like me when I was his age, he hits the ball too high and too hard. He has trouble keeping it low."

In the four years since Daly had won the PGA Championship, Nicklaus had rethought his position on the resemblances between Daly and himself. As Daly's swing became known and admired around the golfing world, Nicklaus got comfortable comparing Daly's swing with his—even if this was folly. Daly didn't merely hit the ball hard, as Nicklaus had; Daly hit it farther than anyone who had ever played the pro tour. Conversely, Nicklaus had won thirty tournaments, including six majors, by the time he was twenty-nine. Daly had won three.

In writing Daly off so quickly at St. Andrews, Nicklaus was forgetting that during a practice round for the 1993 British Open at Royal St. George's, in Kent, England, he had revealed his secret to playing golf in the wind to Daly: If you can't hit the ball low, then allow for the wind. Don't fight it.

It was probably the sole piece of advice Daly ever accepted from Nicklaus—and one of the few suggestions he had ever taken from anyone. Daly had gone out that week and, sometimes aiming thirty yards wide of his intended target, rode his ball on the wind to twelfth place. It was the only instance in his three British Opens that Daly didn't finish last.

The wind was much stronger than that on Sunday at St. Andrews, but the fairways of the Old Course were wide enough for Daly to risk using his driver off the tee for most of his early holes. His second shots to the sometimes narrow and well-bunkered greens required more care. That was where his weeks of practice in Rogers paid off. His short game was sharper than ever, enabling him to punch iron shots under the wind when he needed to.

Having started the day four shots off the lead, Daly birdied three holes on the front nine. Michael Campbell, playing behind him, was getting blown out of the tournament by the wind and his inexperience. He bogeyed three holes on the front side and surrendered the lead to Daly before the turn.

Daly's closest competitor was Costantino Rocca, a thirty-eight-year-old journeyman member of the European PGA Tour. He had done factory work and been a caddie master in Italy before turning pro at twenty-four. In the fourteen succeeding years he had earned over $1 million, but little acclaim, while winning twice on the European tour and six times elsewhere. He was infamous in Europe for having Europe's defeat in the 1993 Ryder Cup competition with the United States blamed on him, because he had lost the deciding match of the tournament.

Rocca had come to the first tee on Sunday in second place, and by late afternoon he was still there, not making a move on Daly but not kindly disappearing from contention, either, as Michael Campbell seemed to be doing. When Daly reached the sixteenth hole, he had a three-shot lead over Rocca, who was playing behind Daly. It wasn't an enormous margin, but it wasn't so small as to be frightening—although that was John Daly's assessment of his situation.

When Daly was cruising to his win in the PGA Championship, it was almost as if he were on a television game show. He was drinking in those days, and that kept him as loose as an overly enthused contestant. More important, the actuality of winning a major golf tournament was so far removed from his experiences, and those of the people around him, that he might as well have been spinning a wheel or answering questions. He knew that he would get a bunch of prizes if he kept doing the right things that afternoon, but the day-to-day impact of winning—not to mention the $30 million contract—exceeded the limits of his imagination. This was a blessing, because it let him play terrific golf, while simultaneously preventing the collar of his shirt from cinching around his neck until he became faint.

The scales had dropped from John Daly's eyes since then. Without picking up any additional sponsors or outings, winning the British Open—between the $200,000 first prize, and the bonus money from his existing contracts—was going to put the better part of a million dollars into his accounts within short order. Really, though, that was a minor part of it, because by now the money was numbers on paper.

Much more imposing to John Daly was the question of whether someone like him was suitable to win the British Open. It wasn't only the licensed betting shops with their sixty-six-to-one odds that told him he was a dark horse; it was everything about this hoary town and this relic-laden tournament. In addition to having the normal European allotment of grand castles and vaulted cathedrals, the hamlet of St. Andrews functioned as a living golf museum. It brimmed with quaint shops selling everything that ever had anything to do with golf—particularly if it could be claimed as antique. With the proper sum of money and reservations, it was possible to actually play the Old Course as presidents and royalty had. The net effect was to be immersed in an imaginary time and a fairy-tale place where one cavorted on the links with one's fellow lords and gentlemen while pledging loyalty to the throne.

John Daly arrived into this setting from the colonies, sporting an especially original coiffure that was the spare-time handiwork of a country-and-western singer, who may have created said haircut in a campground, outside the Daly motor home—almost certainly while wearing cowboy boots. Although Daly took a lot of ribbing about this and other eccentricities from the media, it never interfered with his relationship with his British fans when he was out there busting drives. But now he was standing on the sixteenth tee with the distinct chance of becoming the next British Open champion—and he was freaked.

It was as though Elvis Presley, another man from Memphis, had been invited to perform at La Scala by mistake. After being hustled into the building under cover of darkness, he lounged backstage until moments before the lights went down. Then, sporting a fringed and spangled jumpsuit, he peered from behind the stage curtain and discovered an opulent opera house, its seats filled with people in dandy clothes and glittering jewels.

Given Daly's three-shot lead in the tournament, this was the time for a conservative strategy. By playing carefully—and especially by hitting irons off the tee—he wouldn't score bogeys and give the thing away. This would force Rocca to take unprofitable risks in an effort to gain on him. At least that was the conventional wisdom, which didn't allow for the Presley-at-La Scala effect.

When Daly realized where he was and what might soon happen, the golf equivalent of the view from behind the curtain struck him: He could be humiliated here, simply because of who he was. After that, there were no options. He had to awe them. Elvis would have knocked them out of their seats with blazing renditions of the loosest-hipped songs in his repertoire. John Daly grabbed his driver.

Up in the broadcast booth, Daly's old TV nemesis, Brent Musburger, asked Jack Nicklaus what he thought about Daly standing there with his longest club in his hand. "If I were his caddie," Nicklaus said, "the first thing I'd do is put that driver back in his bag. I can't believe he's going to play that golf club. It's the only way he can lose the golf tournament."

Daly blistered a great drive, then three-putted for bogey. With two holes left for him to play, Daly's lead was cut to two strokes, and the pressure he had been feeling was cubed. Many golfers thought the seventeenth hole at the Old Course was the hardest par four in golf—there was so much trouble strewn about that practically anything could go wrong.

Brent Musburger asked Jack Nicklaus what advice he had for John Daly now. "I think I would hand my driver to someone in the gallery and tell them to give it back to me after number eighteen," Nicklaus said. "I can't imagine him playing more than a one- or two-iron. Probably a two-iron."

Daly pulled his driver from his bag.

"Oh, my gosh," Nicklaus said. "Oh, no."

Daly pulled his tee shot way left into thick knee-high rough. He scrambled out of that, only to plop his ball into one of the most terrifying bunkers on the course. He narrowly escaped from that and two-putted for bogey. Daly's lead was cut to one.

Daly parred the eighteenth hole, then he and Paulette

watched on TV as Costantino Rocca, needing a birdie to tie and force a playoff, nearly reached the eighteenth green with his tee shot. He flubbed his second shot like the rankest of amateurs, leaving himself with an impossible sixty-five-foot putt through an undulating depression in front of the green called the Valley of Sin. Rocca was hoping he could two-putt from there to secure a tie for second with three other players. When his first putt tumbled into the hole, Rocca pitched forward onto the earth and cried, while John Daly closed his eyes and sighed like someone learning he had a fatal illness.

It only took Daly a few seconds to recover from the blow. He knew instantly what he was going to do during the coming four-hole playoff. He would forget everything anyone had ever told him about golf or how to play the Old Course. He would go out there and assault the course with a fury they had never seen in Scotland before. He would play golf the right way—the way he had taught himself to play at the Bay Ridge Boat and Golf Club, when he was small and the world was even more difficult to understand.

There were a couple of dozen people at the Bay Ridge Boat and Golf Club watching John Daly on TV as he reached that decision. They nodded in recognition at the look they saw on their local hero's face. It was the same one that was depicted in a painting that hung in the clubhouse. In the picture, Daly is driving a ball from Bay Ridge into the upper reaches of neighboring Mt. Nebo, much the way that Daly himself had soared from Dardanelle and into the stratosphere.

Jane Witherall could attest to that. She had sometimes played golf with John at Bay Ridge when he first lived in Dardanelle, then she was going to give lessons with him at the Wildcat Hollow Driving Range after John had come back from the South African tour for the first time. Now she was sitting in the Bay Ridge clubhouse with her seventy-eight-year-old mother, and a collection of the faithful, waiting for John to win the British Open.

Jim and Lou Daly were watching at home. John had wanted his father to get a passport and come over to Scotland with John and Paulette, but Jim never did. He was selling real estate, having gotten out of working construction, and he needed to be around for that. You also had that long flight, the strange food and hotels, the money being different and all. John would be at the course all the time, and Jim wouldn't really know anybody. He wouldn't know what to say to people. . . .

Besides, he had to be around in case Lou needed help running the store. John had made it possible for his family to open the Highway 22 Convenience Store and John Daly Golf Shop across the road from Bay Ridge. It sat thirty yards back off the road there, with parking in the front that you could zip into off the east-west route through town. Lou worked in the store with Jamie, who was back in Dardanelle with the family. Jamie had been married for a while, but that didn't work out. Outside the store, he was a volunteer fireman. With Jamie and John's history of partying dating back to Jefferson City, people thought it was best if Jamie didn't travel with John regularly anymore.

Jim and Lou and Jamie were real proud of John out there in the universe beyond Dardanelle, but that wasn't their life. With the store, they had something to keep them busy and generate income. They couldn't get fired, that was for sure. It was good that Jim got out of construction, which was always dicey. Directly or indirectly, most of this stuff was John's doing. Pretty much on his own, he had made things better for everyone at home. That was why they weren't worried about him in the playoff—except maybe Lou, who could get excitable.

Over at Don Cline's house, he was every bit as confident. If anybody wanted to know what Don Cline thought about John

Daly, all Cline had to do was take them up to the second floor, where he maintained his John Daly room. It was a space in his house that was decorated entirely with pictures and memorabilia of John and his career—like a little museum. Cline loved Daly as if he were his own son, and he was sure to be letting out a whoop when that boy won his second major.

With everyone in Dardanelle enthralled with the broadcast of the British Open, they weren't paying a lot of mind to the fast-moving summer thunderstorm whipping through the fields outside of town. Both the temperature and the humidity could push into the nineties in Arkansas in August, making a soaking thunderstorm with a good wind behind it a refreshment that was often welcome. But it was a hellacious storm, sizzling with electricity, that was coming this afternoon. Just as John Daly was about to enjoin Costantino Rocca in a playoff to determine the winner of the 124th British Open Championship—*crack!* A massive bolt of lightning struck the earth in Dardanelle and cut the power to half the buildings in town.

The support John Daly was receiving in St. Andrews was not as unanimous as it was in Dardanelle. Some of that was Europeans backing a member of their tour. But there were also Americans in the locker room who were pulling for Rocca, such was their free-floating scorn for Daly. Daly didn't mind, for outside his circle of personal friends, he had been at odds with the world before. Having people wish him ill was just another day.

Daly didn't have time for any of this crap with the playoff about to start. He stroked his putter and whipped some clubs around, thinking only about how he was going to crush this man who was trespassing in his dream. Then three American golfers, Corey Pavin, Brad Faxon, and Bob Estes, stopped for a moment to offer Daly encouragement. At first Daly worried that he must be looking troubled—or weak—for the men to have made those gestures. Then another American, Mark

Brooks, rushed into the locker room to get a yardage book for the course after Daly couldn't find his, and Daly understood there were people on the tour who were ready to be his friends.

Daly pushed that out of his mind and, with fierceness radiating from him, headed for his showdown. He parred the first hole but went one stroke up because Rocca three-putted. Daly picked up another stroke on the second hole with a thirty-five-foot birdie putt. The playoff jumped to the notorious seventeenth hole then, where Daly had barely escaped with a bogey during regulation play.

As the golfers were getting into position, Daly's support staff in Dardanelle was coming back on line. Don Cline still had his electricity, but the lightning had blown out his downstairs TV. He only had to go upstairs to the John Daly room, where he kept a small black and white set. He was watching the finale there, surrounded by his souvenirs.

The electricity was out at the Bay Ridge Boat and Golf Club, and Jane Witherall hustled her elderly mother out to the car and shot down Route 22 looking for a house with the lights on. When she saw one, she took her mother up, pounded on the stranger's door, and asked to come in. This was Dardanelle, after all, and anyone not watching John Daly in the British Open needed some encouragement.

Jim and Lou Daly hurried out to their car, too, but they used a cellular phone to call ahead to Wanda Ferguson, who had come over to Wildcat Hollow for a while on the day four years ago when John had won the PGA Championship. Wanda was in and had electricity. Lou and Jim sped to her house, arriving about the time John was preparing to tee off on the seventeenth hole—with his driver.

"He's got the driver again!" Jack Nicklaus said into his microphone with exasperation. He could only wonder when this young man was going to learn to be more like Jack Nicklaus. Then he seemed to realize that the answer would have to be expressed in millenniums.

Nicklaus also understood there was something else he had to say, with millions of people watching around the world, but that didn't mean he had to like it.

"Well," he said, finally, "he's in the playoff. I'm not."

Daly creamed a drive down the fairway, then knocked a nine-iron onto the green, twenty feet from the pin. Rocca also used his driver, but, playing catch-up, he plopped his second shot into the Road Bunker and took three strokes to get out. Not long afterward, the silversmith who carves the winner's name on the tournament's famous claret-jug trophy began his work.

The bleachers on each side of the eighteenth green were at capacity, and more people were watching from the clubhouse that ran between the stands. They know their history in St. Andrews, and everyone was aware that Daly was about to become only the fourth man since the war to win two majors before he turned thirty. After he hit a nice two-iron off the tee, the spectators gave Daly a thunderous ovation as he approached the eighteenth green. With two putts from Daly, it was over. The spectators cheered again, and Paulette came running out.

Daly looked numb and distracted as he walked through the trophy ceremony, thanking everyone and saying how pleased he was. He almost cried when he looked at the trophy and saw his name listed among those of the most-accomplished people who had ever played the game. It was hard for Daly to fully grasp where he had arrived, and given the jaggedness of his journey, how he had survived to get there.

He had billed his success in Atlanta in 1994 as his first victory while sober. But his conquest of St. Andrews, coming after seven months of subdued behavior, was his first win while test-certified alcohol-free.

To have grown up in Dardanelle and gone through all he

had experienced, only to win the British Open at twenty-nine, was far more than Daly could ever explain to the media, so he didn't even try. He went to the pressroom with Paulette and told the reporters that he was pretty sure he probably loved his wife more than golf. "To have a child that we have here is incredible," he said. "And she better get ready to have more, because I am going to get a boy."

Paulette was smiling away in the back, talking about John Daly after alcohol. "He's quite content now," she said. "He doesn't show me it's a daily battle. Oh, he brings it up once in a while, about wanting a drink, but not very often anymore. He's so different from when I first met him."

John was telling reporters the same thing. "I think I just had a lot of problems dealing with things that weren't on the golf course," he said. "I wasn't very mature, and I think drinking had a lot to do with that. I don't think I would be here today if I were still drinking.

"I made some stupid decisions. I'm trying my ass off to regain a lot of friendships. I am trying to do everything I can in my life off the golf course to make sure that I have a happy life."

For the second time in four years, Bill Clinton was going to call John Daly, only now he was the president of the United States rather than the governor of Arkansas. Jay Leno had replaced Johnny Carson on the *Tonight Show,* and this time Daly was going to accept their invitation to come. If only to demonstrate that he was still a little crazy, Daly was going to shave his head again in a few weeks.

All of this was wonderful, but none of it could give Daly the closure he needed with someone who had seen him through the incredibly gritty reality of it all—the six-mile march from the totaled Blazer, one potentially fatal overdose after another, the humiliating and very public arrest. Only someone who had been immersed in the nightmares could fully grasp what it meant for John Daly to win the British Open.

Daly found a telephone and punched in the number for the house at Wildcat Hollow. Lou and Jim had been expecting the call, and they had dashed home from Wanda Ferguson's to be there waiting when it arrived. Jim was going to kid his boy about his father's not having come to the tournament and tell John that he would have lost, sure as hell, if Jim had been there.

But Lou grabbed the phone first, and when she put it to her ear she could hear John saying, "Mom," and it sounded like he was crying.

Lou didn't want her boy to have to say anything else with his voice all weak and choked up like that, especially at a time like this, so she cut him off. There was only one thing her John needed to hear. "Son," she said, the way a mother does, pre-empting all others. "Son, you did wonderful."